THE KOBE HOTEL

OTHER BOOKS BY MASAYA SAITO

HAIKU

Ash (TELS Press, 1988)
Snow Bones (Isobar Press, 2016)

TRANSLATIONS

Sanki Saitō, *The Kobe Hotel* (1st edition: Weatherhill, 1993)
Sanki Saitō, *Selected Haiku 1933–1962* (Isobar Press, 2023)

THE KOBE HOTEL

MEMOIRS

Sanki Saitō

translated and with an introduction by

Masaya Saito

ISOBAR PRESS

First edition (including haiku) published in 1993 by Weatherhill.

Second, revised edition (without haiku and with a new introduction) published in 2023 by

Isobar Press
Sakura 2-21-23-202, Setagaya-ku,
Tokyo 156-0053, Japan

&

14 Isokon Flats, Lawn Road,
London NW3 2XD, United Kingdom

https://isobarpress.com

ISBN 978-4-907359-45-4

Translations and introduction © Masaya Saito 1993, 2023

All rights reserved.

COVER PHOTOGRAPHS

FRONT: Nakayama Iwate, *Tor Road, Kobe*, 1939. BACK: unknown USAAF photographer, incendiary bombs falling on Kobe, 4 June 1945.

Contents

Introduction / 7

KOBE

The Story of the Strange Egyptian / 27
A Woman Called Namiko / 34
The Brave Sailor and the Taiwanese / 43
Black Bread and Death / 51
The Go-Between / 58
The German Shepherd / 66
Journey by Car / 73
The Night-Blind Gentleman / 81
Parboiling Shark / 89
The Cat-Crazy Cuckold / 99

KOBE SEQUEL

Preface / 108
About a Lady / 109
Three Maidens / 117
Haiku Once Again / 126
A Story of Sounding Sirens / 134
Like a Rolling Stone / 142

Translator's Acknowledgments / 151

A NOTE ON JAPANESE NAMES

Throughout this book Japanese names are printed in the customary Japanese order with family name first, except in the case of Saitō Sanki, whose name on the cover and the title page is printed in the English-language order for the convenience of booksellers and librarians.

Sanki and other haiku poets are initially referred to in this book by both of their names (family name followed by given name), but thereafter – as is usual in Japan for haiku poets – by their second (that is, given) name. Thus Matsuo Bashō, for example, is simply referred to as Bashō.

A macron, indicating a double-length vowel, has been added to names where appropriate as an aid to pronunciation.

INTRODUCTION

In the introduction to Sanki Saitō's *Selected Haiku* (published in conjunction with this present volume), I quote from Yoshida Hokushūshi, a haiku poet: 'Sanki was a unique author with a rich inner world, who could be discussed in terms of two disparate categories: "Sanki the person" and "Sanki the writer."'[1] In that introduction, I focus particularly on Sanki the writer; therefore, in this introduction, I should probably refer more to Sanki the person. This is something that the reader, hopefully, can clearly sense when engaging with the main body of this book, so let me limit my introduction here to those years from Sanki's childhood to the start of his Kobe days, where his autobiographical memoirs can take over and speak for themselves.

I SANKI'S PRE-HAIKU DAYS

Saitō Sanki was born Saitō Keichoku on May 15, 1900, in the old castle town of Tsuyama, Okayama prefecture. His father was a school superintendent and an amateur calligrapher, painter, sculptor, and poet. His mother was the daughter of a high-ranking samurai retainer. Their only daughter had died the same year Sanki was born, and consequently he was raised with much affection as the reincarnation of his sister. He also had two older brothers, Takeo and Yasuhiko, who were older than Sanki by twenty and ten years respectively. Following the death of his father when Sanki was six, he and his mother were supported by the eldest son, Takeo, who lived in Tokyo.

In October of 1918, when Sanki was eighteen, his mother died and Takeo became his guardian. Sanki moved to Tokyo, where he was enrolled at the middle school of Aoyama Gakuin, a Methodist school. In 1920, he went on to the high school of the same institution but, in September, dropped out. In 1921, despite a desire to attend art school to study painting, he chose a more practical career in dentistry following his elder brother's advice and, in April, entered Nippon Dental College. During his years at the school, Sanki sought diversion by joining a horse-riding club, and was so taken with social dancing that he eventually acquired a dancing teacher's license.

In September of 1923, the Great Kantō Earthquake devastated Tokyo and its neighboring areas, causing not only severe damage to all different kinds of infrastructure but also more than 105,000 fatalities. We don't know if he was in Tokyo when the disaster happened, and if he was, how he survived it, as the 1923 section of Sanki's own chronological record is blank. However, we do know that at that time Sanki was still enrolled as a student at Nippon Dental College even if he was not studying seriously. Maeda Isamu, who was Sanki's classmate at the college, wrote that 'thanks to the unprecedented scale of the earthquake and the chaos which ensued, [Sanki] was allowed to progress to the senior academic year.'[2]

In April, 1925, Sanki finished college and in November the same year, despite a string of previous romances, he married Uehara Shigeko. The newlyweds were invited to sail to Singapore by Takeo, who was then a manager at the Singapore branch of the NYK Line, Japan's largest shipping company. Takeo intended to save Sanki from his previously licentious life by offering him a fresh start in a new country. Sanki established a dental practice on Orchard Avenue, the main street, in premises that Takeo had bought for the couple as a gift, and which were also their home.

In those days Singapore was under British control, and had a decidedly international flavor. In the 1934 section of Sanki's own chronological record, he states: 'During the daytime, I was immersed in playing golf and, at night, I hung out with my friends from the Near East, to whose mother countries I was afire with high hopes of emigrating, though I did not for lack of courage. At the same time, I ordered books of classical literature from Japan and, fully absorbed, would pore over them.'[3]

While he often closed his dental clinic in order to play golf, at other times the clinic was open, but as a dancehall. Mita Yukio, who was Sanki's close friend in those days, tells us how this came about:

> Licensed as a teacher of social dancing, his skill was great. I remember at a dance party sponsored by the Viceroy and held at the Raffles Hotel, Mr. and Mrs. Saitō's Argentine tango won the championship. As a result of this, Japanese residents, including the consul general and his wife, the managers of all the banks and business firms and their wives, and even young bachelors began to crowd his clinic to beg him for dancing lessons. The floor of the spacious room next to the medical office was polished and was finally made into a superb ballroom.[4]

Sanki had never told Takeo that he was so involved in dancing, but the news of the Saito's dancing triumph was splashed across a Shanghai English-language newspaper and caught the attention of Takeo. Sanki was rebuked by his brother, who assumed that his younger sibling was on the verge of forgetting about his profession – which was, in fact, correct. Eventually the Saitōs went bankrupt. Sanki's debts were taken over by Takeo and a return to Japan was inescapable.

Back in Japan in December 1928, Sanki again opened a dental clinic, this time with financial assistance from his other brother, Yasuhiko. In April 1929 his son, Tarō, was born. The clinic was to be closed in 1932, probably because Sanki lacked the necessary sense of vocation. Nevertheless, before long he had to join the staff of a hospital in Kanda, Tokyo, as the head of its dental department, in order to support his family financially.

He found himself to be 'an unreliable, unconscientious department head', and having been charmed by the equatorial climes of the country he had left, he felt himself to be 'a ghost-like alien' in Tokyo.[5] However, it was at this hospital that he first became closely acquainted with haiku. One day, a urologist approached Sanki and asked him to contribute to his mimeographed haiku publication which was circulated inside the hospital. Although Sanki had been a lover of literature since his childhood, he had no interest in haiku, which he felt to be 'antiquated stuff,'[6] and at first refused the urologist's request. However, his colleague's patients, who were there for the treatment of their venereal diseases, invited themselves to Sanki's consultation room one after another in an effort to persuade him. Sanki finally agreed. He recalled in his autobiograophy, *Haiku Folly*, 'This is the way bad luck trapped me quite by chance, with foul gonorrhea germs as a go-between.'[7]

2 SANKI'S EARLY CAREER AS A HAIKU POET AND THE NEW RISING HAIKU

It was in 1938 that Sanki adopted the pen name, Saitō Sanki, for his haiku. He comments that his pen name (Saitō, written with the characters for West and East, and Sanki, meaning 'three demons') is 'odd'; he goes on to say:

> I'm often asked where it comes from. It was over the telephone I first used this pen name. When the facilitator [for the mimeographed circular], who was a young furniture dealer, was preparing the first print, he called me at the hospital and said, 'All haiku poets have pen names, Doc, so make one for yourself. I'm cutting the stencil now.' In response, I immediately answered 'Sanki' without thinking too much.... According to Takaya Sōshū's theory, 'Sanki' refers to 'drinking, gambling, and buying women.' This cannot be regarded as entirely unfounded – and yet what an unreasonable thing to say.[8]

Sanki never clarified the significance of his pen name. 'Saitō,' pronounced the same as his family name but composed of different characters, may refer to his cosmopolitan nature. As for 'Sanki', he himself wrote that it derives from the English phrase 'Thank you'.[9] The prominent critic of Japanese literature, Yamamoto Kenkichi, explains the motivation behind Sanki's initiation into haiku as follows:

> From the very start, he was never drawn to the traditional shades embedded in haiku and tanka, or rather, to those inherent in the Japanese language itself. A few years of living in Singapore seemed to have instilled in him a mindset reminiscent of those who have lost their homeland or gone into exile.... In relation to the Japanese lifestyle, the Japanese language, and the poetic form known as haiku, Sanki must have approached them with a sensation akin to that of *l'étranger* (a foreigner). But this sense of estrangement is itself the wellspring of vitality in his composition. He discovered that the brief and eccentric seventeen-syllable poetic form, arranged in a 5-7-5 pattern, would bear up as he went on conducting various experimental poetic endeavors, trying to express his not necessarily cheerful inner world. Thus, he attempts to test the possibilities of haiku, while being seized by a curiosity more intense than any other haiku poet's[10]

Despite the fact that it was common practice (and often still is) for a haiku poet to become a disciple of a master, Sanki refused to confine himself to any clique. Traditionally, haiku has been taught in an atmosphere that is, in a sense, feudalistic; that is, a master generally asserts his or her power as the selector of haiku they personally prefer in a *kukai*, a haiku meeting. In contrast, for Sanki, who could obey nothing other than his own poetic sensitivities, it must have been quite natural to regard haiku as a form of literature intended for self-expression, or indeed something deeper than that, rather than as a means of propagating traditional styles or of diverting oneself with a strictly regulated pastime. He showed little or no interest in following any haiku master's sense of values. Having never been infected with traditionalism, he was fortunate enough to be able to push forward with the creation of haiku the like of which no one had ever tried to create.

In the 1934 section of Sanki's own chronological record, he states:

> In January, I joined the haiku journal *Sōmato* (Revolving Lantern). I was a member of this group along with Shimizu Shōshi, Mitani Akira, Hataya Shōkankyo, among others. This year was the period of the sudden surge of the New Rising Haiku. I poured all my energy and time into it. Non-seasonal haiku were [first] advocated by the haiku journal *Amanogawa* (The Milky Way). Appealing to the kindred spirits of Tokyo-based New Rising Haiku magazines such as *Dojō* (On the Soil), *Ku to Hyōron* (Haiku and Criticism), *Waseda Haiku*, and *Sōmato*, I founded the *Shin Haiwa Kai* (New Haiku Discussion Association) as a haiku community network. We began our research in the form of discussion meetings. With this as a starting point, an exchange among the periodicals in the various different areas flourished.[11]

All these haiku poets and groups mentioned above were strongly dissatisfied with traditional haiku and were anxious for a new direction. This enthusiastic rebellion against traditionalism was closely related to the gloomy course of events during the late 1920s and 1930s, during which Japan, like other countries, suffered from the emergence of social and economic difficulties caused by the Great Depression following the Wall Street Crash of 1929. Japan tried to alleviate this disruption to the social order by the invasion of China, which eventually led to the war against the Allied Forces during the Pacific War, which started in 1941.

As regards the relationship between this course of events and the New Rising Haiku, Kanda Hideo points out:

> In 1933, Japan was admonished by the League of Nations and urged to withdraw its troops from Manchuria, but refused to do so, and instead seceded from the League.... [Within Japan] novels had already been suppressed, and poetry also restrained. In times like this, even writers who were not formerly interested in composing haiku joined the haiku-writing community. Thus, their unconscious dissatisfaction with reality ended up being directed towards the conservative views on haiku of Kyoshi [an esteemed but very traditional poet of the time].... The New Rising Haiku movement, thus fermented, spread like wildfire, I think. That is to say that from an historical perspective, the irony of the New Rising Haiku lies in the fact that, in contrast to the Japanese social and cultural environment that gradually began to tend towards seclusion, it tried to insist on an opposing tendency towards the liberation and expansion of haiku.[12]

Although the movement coincided with the period when Japan was heading towards the Second World War, most of the poets involved had spent their childhood and youth during a relatively peaceful era, that is to say, during the Taishō period (1912–26) and the early years of the following Shōwa period. These years were not only relatively peaceful but also saw Japan's rapid modernization, especially in urban areas. For instance, Tokyo's landscape changed drastically, especially after the great Kantō Earthquake in 1923, as Edwin O. Reischauer explains:

> Downtown Tokyo became a city of wide thoroughfares and steel and reinforced concrete buildings, with sections resembling the cities of Europe and America more than those of Asia. The Marunouchi district around Tokyo's main railway station became the pride of the nation and a symbol

of the new Japan. Other cities followed Tokyo's lead. Modern office buildings, school buildings, large movie houses, great stadiums, and sprawling railway stations became the typical architecture of urban Japan. The morning newspaper, long daily commuting by train and streetcar between home and office, and the quick break for lunch came to typify a new urban style.[13]

It was indeed huge shifts in technology and culture such as these that many of the rebellious poets had the chance to witness. Thus, they nurtured a strong desire to create haiku in tune with the zeitgeist, while refusing to blindly follow the traditional, nature-oriented aesthetics represented through language based upon objective observation.

3 THE AUTHORITARIAN OPPRESSION OF THE NEW RISING HAIKU MOVEMENT

In 1934, Sanki began submitting his haiku to *Amanogawa* (Milky Way), whose editor was Yoshioka Zenjidō, a New Rising Haiku poet who had formerly been one of Kyoshi's disciples, but who was ejected from the Hototogisu group because he became an exponent of haiku without seasonal words.

In addition, in the spring of 1935, the leader of Kyōdai Haiku, Hirahata Seitō, eagerly invited Sanki to join his New Rising Haiku group, which was based at Kyoto University. Sanki soon cut a brilliant figure in this group, which under his influence grew from being a mere publisher of a campus magazine into the most radical and active of all the strongholds of the New Rising Haiku groups. With *Kyōdai Haiku* as his main literary base, Sanki published a stream of haiku, and soon came to be regarded as the standard-bearer of the New Rising Haiku.

In November the same year, he became bedridden with tuberculosis. During his illness he had time to reflect on his previous failures and frustrations, and resolved to devote himself to haiku. It was at this time that he produced one of his masterpieces. Indeed, the following haiku is even inscribed on Sanki's gravestone within the grounds of Jōdōji Temple in Tsuyama City.

水枕ガバリと寒い海がある
mizu-makura gabari-to samui umi ga aru

My rubber pillow
sloshes –
the cold sea
(first published in the March 1936 issue of *Amanogawa*)

A 'mizu-makura' (translated above as 'rubber pillow') is sometimes still used for the purpose of cooling the back of a sick person's head. It is made of rubber, usually a reddish brown in color, and is filled with iced water. The adverbial phrase 'gabari-to' is onomatopoeic. This phrase is usually used to conjure up the state or sound of vigorously rising waves or other things. In this poem, the wave suddenly billows in Sanki's dreamy and feverish consciousness. Suzuki Murio says of this poem:

> A high fever caused by pulmonary infiltrate persisted. [Sanki] had death in mind, and thus came up with the word 'cold' – it is anxiety itself. This haiku has been seen as the one which marks Sanki's epiphany regarding haiku; it opened up to him new possibilities by introducing surreal imagery.[14]

Upon recovery, Sanki quit his dental practice and began working for a small commercial firm owned by Mita Yukio, with whom he had become acquainted during his Singapore days. He was entrusted with buying and selling, but goods were scarce and business was poor.

In July 1937, the Second Sino-Japanese War broke out. New

Rising Haiku poets, including Tomizawa Kakio and Hashimoto Mudō, departed for battlefronts and composed haiku there. But Sanki and some other members of Kyōdai Haiku, who had not yet been drafted, devoted themselves to the composition of so called 'senka-sōbō haiku'; haiku which described the horrors of war, but which were based upon the poet's imagination, or often, upon newsreels, newspaper articles and photographs. The following are only a few examples of the many written by Sanki:

血が冷ゆる夜の土から茸生え
chi ga hiyuru yoru no tsuchi kara kinoko hae

Blood cools
on the night earth
where mushrooms grow
(published in the November 1937 issue of *Kyōdai Haiku*)

パラシウト天地の機銃フト黙ル
parashūto tenchi no kijū futo damaru

A parachute –
in the sky and on the earth
hushed machine guns
(published in the May 1938 issue of *Kyōdai Haiku*)

絶叫する高度一万の若い戦死
zekkyō suru kōdo ichiman no wakai senshi

Screaming
at 10,000 feet
an early death in battle
(published in the December 1939 issue of *Kyōdai Haiku*)

Traditionalists frowned upon senka-sōbō haiku. To them, the act of composing war haiku while remaining on the home front was utterly disrespectful to those soldiers fighting on the battlefields. Furthermore, to them, a war haiku devoid of a season word (like the second and third examples) was no longer a haiku. In an essay titled 'Kyōdai Haiku and Saitō Sanki', Hirahata Seitō recollects:

> After Sanki joined our Kyōdai Haiku, it drastically changed. We fully opened our gates to liberalists throughout the whole world of haiku; furthermore, we had a period when we were regarded as the Mecca of the New Rising Haiku, due to the intellectual sophistication of our works. It was a period that used to be called the war haiku era. That brilliance, in which anti-war haiku and war-weary haiku followed one after another, was something that could have been attained only by us, the group of liberalists, with Sanki as its head. It was natural that we came to be subjected to strong criticism from the world of traditional haiku, and that we gradually found ourselves attracting attention from the secret police; yet my memory of those few years, when I was in the midst of this maelstrom, remains vivid and fresh.[15]

In the last paragraph of the same essay, Seitō also writes:

> This is just a supposition, but I wonder what would have happened to Sanki if Kyōdai Haiku had not existed. It is quite natural to assume of course, that Saitō Sanki would have existed as a prominent poet. But it is doubtful at least that he would have created those brilliant and sad anti-war haiku. I claim this because the atmosphere, which encouraged Sanki to compose war haiku, was something unique to this group.[16]

In 1940, the Special Higher Police arrested members of Kyōdai

Haiku on three different dates: eight members (including Seitō) on February 14; six members (including Ishibashi Tatsunosuke, Mitani Akira, and Watanabe Hakusen) on May 3; finally, Sanki on August 31, all under charges of violating the Peace Preservation Law. This law was originally put in force in 1925 to crack down on those supporting the abolition of the imperial system and capitalism. To put it more succinctly, the law tried to outlaw communism. The critic Yamamoto Kenkichi refers to the arrest of the New Rising Haiku poets in these terms:

> With the Old Left having been crushed, so-called liberalists came to be regarded as the new extreme left wing. The Special Higher Police conspired to have them arrested on false charges of breaking the Peace Preservation Law and, thus, justify their own raison d'etre. This was an inevitable abuse due to the bureaucracy within a militaristic state and was proof of the corruption at its heart. Indeed, it was not the case that their haiku had the power of resistance ascribed to it. With lack of more targets to crack down on, the secret police arrested innocent citizens as they pleased and, in this way, prevented their own positions from becoming dispensable and so secured their jobs. A mass arrest, which began with the Kyōdai Haiku New Rising Haiku poets, was a heinous act by the authorities, who fabricated a reason for it where there was none. New Rising Haiku poets were their poor victims.[17]

After being detained in a jail cell for about seventy days, Sanki's indictment was revoked and he was allowed to return home, though he was forbidden to write.

In late 1942, Sanki permanently left his wife and son, moving from Tokyo to the large port city of Kobe. There, he took up residence in a rundown hotel that housed a number of foreigners and also women who worked in Kobe's bars. Though officially robbed of haiku by the authorities, he lived a bohemian life, which later fermented into the narratives of *Kobe* and *Kobe Sequel*.

My introduction has now reached the point where Sanki's memoirs begin. So here I will stop narrating any further biographical details in order to allow his own words to take up the story of his next few years. Before that, however, let me give a few details about the publishing history and reception of the book whose translation you are about to read.

5 THE RECEPTION AND CHARACTERISTICS OF *KOBE*

Kobe was serialized in *Haiku*, the general haiku magazine published by Kadokawa Shoten, from September 1954 until June 1956, while *Kobe Sequel* was serialized in *Tenrō* (Dog Star), the haiku periodical Sanki started with Yamaguchi Seishi as its head, from August 1959 until December 1959. Since these original appearances, both of these autobiographical essays have been published together as a single book (sometimes together with other Sanki works) in no less than six different editions, starting with *Kobe, Zoku Kobe, Haigu-den* (Kobe, Kobe Sequel, Haiku Folly) published by Shuppan-sha in 1975. The most recent edition is *Kobe, Zoku Kobe* (Kobe, Kobe Sequel) published by Shinchosha in 2019. The publication history of the two works in so many different editions demonstrates their obvious and lasting appeal to a large readership.

Itsuki Hiroyuki, a famed novelist and essayist, wrote the blurb for the 1975 edition, giving it the title 'In Admiration of *Kobe*':

> There have been many literary works which portray the misery of war head on, and also more than a few which reflect the tragedy of defeat in war. However, I doubt that, except for this *Kobe* by Mr. Saitō, there has been any other which depicts the turbulent era in such a unique manner

and emits such strange exoticism and romanticism. With the reverberance of the heavy basso continuo of fascism in the background, he honestly describes his days when he lived with a group of people at the lowest depth of society; thus, *Kobe* could become a rare testimony of those times. It is one of my great joys of this year that this renowned work has finally seen the light of day. I have no doubt that this is a masterpiece which will remain in the history of Shōwa literature.[18]

What is it that makes this 'masterpiece' so popular, to the point where it has been repeatedly published in several different editions over the last sixty years? There is no clear and simple answer to this question. Could it be because of Sanki's reputation as a haiku poet? Could it be because of his unassuming candor and unfettered diction? Could it be because of the offbeat setting in which these Japanese ne'er-do-wells and expatriates find themselves: a disheveled hotel in wartime Kobe? Could it be the characters, whom he observes with empathy but also with a certain distance? Could it be because of the human dramas involving pathos, tinges of humor and irony, which lend deep insight into human existence? Could it be a sense of solace which readers gain by seeing others, like themselves, experiencing worldly turmoil?

Indeed, all of these can be reasons for *Kobe*'s large readership. However, although the core reason, if any, is yet to be pinpointed, it could in fact have been identified by Sanki himself. In the preface for *Kobe Sequel*, he says:

> All those people who appear in *Kobe* are good people, whether Japanese or not; at the same time, they are the people farthest away from 'a wartime state of emergency.' Like them, I too believed that freedom, and nothing else, was the highest reason for living and, therefore, had a deep interest in their ways of living.[19]

Isn't this strong sense of freedom the primary reason for the popularity of *Kobe*? The current translator believes so. Freedom is something human beings in general constantly seek, and is something none of us can live without; a point Sanki made all those years ago through his prose works such as *Kobe* and *Kobe Sequel*, among others, and, of course, through his 'sophisticated poetry' – which, as Donald Keene observed, is 'not directly connected to any tradition of modern haiku'.[20]

Above all, this is quintessentially what Sanki was: a poet who embodied freedom.

Masaya Saito
Tokyo, August 2023

NOTES

1 Yoshida Hokushūshi, 'Ningen Saitō Sanki' [Saitō Sanki the Person], *Haiku Kenkyū* [Haiku Studies] 38, no. 4 (April 1971): 105.
2 Maeda Isamu, 'Sanki Aoyama Gakuin Jidai no Tsuioku' [Sanki: My Memoirs of His Aoyama Gakuin Days], *Haiku* 11, no. 7 (July 1962): 105.
3 Saitō Sanki, 'Jihitsu Nempu' [My Own Chronological Record] in *Saitō Sanki Zen Kushū* [The Collected Haiku of Saitō Sanki] (Kadokawa, 2018), 406.
4 Mita Yukio, 'Saitō Keichoku no Koto' [Things about 'Saitō Keichoku], *Haiku* 11, no. 5 (May 1962): 60–62.
5 Saitō Sanki, 'Haiguden 1: Waga Tōku Jidai' [My Haiku Submission Days], *Haiku* 8, no. 5 (April 1959): 30.
6 Ibid., 31.
7 Ibid., 31.
8 Ibid., 31–33.
9 Quoted by Suzuki Murio in Suzuki Murio and Sawaki Kin'ichi, *Shintei Haiku Shiriizu – Hito to Sakuhin* 13, *Saitō Sanki* [Revised Haiku Series – Authors and Their Works 13, Saitō Sanki] (Ōfusha, 1979), 17.
10 Yamamoto Kenkichi, *Gendai Haiku* [Modern Haiku] (Kadokawa, 1984), 395.
11 Saitō Sanki, 'Jihitsu Nenpu' [My Own Chronological Record], 407.
12 Kanda Hideo, 'Saitō Sanki Kanken' [My Limited Perspective on Sanki], *Haiku* 11, no. 5 (May 1962): 24.
13 Reischauer, Edwin O., *Japan: The Story of a Nation*, Third ed. (Charles E. Tuttle, 1990), 173.
14 Suzuki Murio, *Kyakuchū Meiku Shiriizu: Saitō Sanki Shū* [A Collection of Famous Haiku with Footnotes: Saitō Sanki Collection] (Haijin-Kyōkai, 1994), 6.
15 Hirahata Seitō, 'Kyōdai Haiku' and Saitō Sanki, *Haiku Kenkyū* 38, no. 4 (April 1971): 88–89.
16 Ibid., 89.

17 Yamamoto Kenkichi, *Gendai Haiku* [Modern Haiku] (Kadokawa, 1984), 33.

18 Itsuki Hiroyuki, blurb for *Kobe / Zoku-Kobe / Haiguden* [Kobe / Kobe Sequel / Haiku Folly] (Shuppan-sha, 1975).

19 Saitō Sanki, *Kobe / Zoku-Kobe* [Kobe / Kobe Sequel] (Shinchōsha, 2019).

20 Keene, Donald, *Dawn to the West: Japanese Literature of the Modern Era: Poetry, Drama, Criticism* (Holt, Rinehart & Winston, 1984), 171.

KOBE

THE STORY OF THE STRANGE EGYPTIAN

In the winter of 1942 I deserted everything I had ever known in Tokyo, and on a certain evening found myself descending a hillside street in the port city of Kobe. A cold buffeting wind from the sea assaulted the mountain slopes behind the city, yet my heart was filled with the knowledge that I had finally freed myself from my former life.

I also knew that somehow I had to find a reasonable apartment that very same evening. Past experience in Tokyo had taught me that by going into any bar I could usually find a single woman living in an apartment. I walked slowly down the hill, my face buried deep in the collar of my overcoat. Ahead of me – I do not know from which corner she appeared – a woman with the look of a bar hostess was hurrying along as though to escape the cold. I tracked her like a hound. As I had expected, she entered a bar near Sannomiya Station, and I slipped in after her. An hour later, I had learned from her of a hotel that also served as an apartment house.

It was a strange hotel. In the middle of Kobe, painted red like some cheap theatre, the hotel stood halfway up Tor Road (then called Tor Doro as English was frowned upon during World War II), which runs straight down to the sea. I was a long-term guest until the air raids began, along with various other people who remained rooted there. The residents were twelve Japanese, a White Russian woman, a Turkish-Tartar couple, an Egyptian man, a Taiwanese man, and a Korean woman. Among the twelve Japanese, two were men: myself and a middle-aged hospital director; the others were either madams or their employees.

These women lived on the canned goods and black bread brought by the German sailors from the submarines and cargo ships harbored in Kobe. They never brought men into their own rooms, though, for such behavior was considered slovenly and invited contempt from their group.

I was a salesman at the time, but those under the same roof, including the foreigners (the German sailors, too), called me Sensei, a title of respect meaning 'teacher,' for a reason that will become clear later in this memoir.

The women brought to this sensei's room many kinds of immediate problems, while the foreigners, under the watchful eye of the alien registration department of the prefectural office, brought subtle problems related to their wartime status.

My business was to supply munitions manufacturers with miscellaneous materials, but, because of the great shortage of commodities, business was terribly slow. I was always poor and spent most of the day sitting with my chin in my hands, watching passers-by from an upstairs window facing Tor Road.

A mysterious crazy man would appear beneath my window every three days or so. He was tall and seemed to be homeless. Upon reaching his favorite spot, even when the cold wind blew, he would take off almost everything he wore and, clad only in his loincloth and standing upright with arms crossed, he would stare into the heavens. Then, balanced on his left heel, he would begin to rotate, spinning rapidly like a living top. Once, when our eyes met, while his were gazing toward the sky and mine were staring down from the window, he called out, 'Hello.'

I asked him why he was spinning around like that.

'This calms my disturbed heart,' was his reply.

When I asked him whether he felt cold, he said, 'I'm cooling myself down.' In effect, he was simply expressing himself freely, as the rest of us wished we could have done.

Sometimes, he would suggest politely, 'Wouldn't you like to come down and join me?' But my head would always remain resting in my hands.

After sustaining this activity for some twenty minutes, he would dress himself again and walk quietly away in his rags, leaving behind a sense of desolation reminiscent of the wasteland described by John the Baptist. Two years later, countless incendiary bombs rained down from the heavens onto his favorite spot and throughout the city, and as a result, tens of thousands of civilians similarly gyrated as they were being stripped naked by the flames.

One of the boarders, Mr. Maged Elba, became my close friend. He was one of only two Egyptians living in Japan at that time. Though he was a civilian of a so-called hostile country, he had almost complete freedom, at least in Kobe, although, like all French, English, and Americans who had not been repatriated, he was not allowed to travel outside the city limits.

Maged was the strangest person in this strange hotel. He was a butcher by trade and had a clean shop on a street uptown, but already it was impossible to keep it stocked. As he disliked living alone at the shop, he went out of his way to reside at the hotel.

How old was he? I could never tell, but I imagine he was around forty. His light brown, finely chiseled face always showed a trace of blue after shaving. His chest was incredibly robust, resembling a wooden barrel. Unlike most wanderers of this type, his spoken English and Japanese were rather poor, although he had been living in Japan for ten years. After wandering through Europe, the United States, and South America, he had finally taken root in Kobe – a strong Egyptian-born reed.

I had spent my youth in Singapore, which was then a British equatorial colony, so I could understand his cosmopolitan nature. The tall tales he told about his native land seemed to spring from his name, Elba, which was not only the island of Napoleon's exile, but was also apparently his own place of birth. Every time he told the story, it seemed as if he could be an illegitimate son of Napoleon.

Both Maged and I were poor, so at night we would usually smoke quietly in either his room or mine. I had about a dozen phonograph records in my room. My collection consisted of Middle Eastern and African music, which had been the inspiration of my dreams since my youth.

Sometimes we would sit together late into the night, slowly sipping beer Maged had somehow managed to lay his hands on. As we played record after record, Maged would become so excited that he would begin to dance wildly, filled with some uncontrollable emotion. Conjured up in his mind, I imagined, were images of an oasis, a caravan of camels, and an old woman selling her wares in a Persian market. Naturally, I would applaud feverishly.

What sort of god was watching over us? It must have been one of the pagan gods, and not a first-rate one at that.

Speaking of gods, Maged was a Muslim, and a very strict observer of the doctrines of his religion. He once developed a high fever during an attack of periodontitis and was finally admitted to a hospital. As a favour to my close friend, I would cook a meal once a day and carry it to him on my bicycle.

One day, I fixed mashed potatoes and thoughtlessly threw some chopped bacon into the recipe. When I placed it at his bedside, he gave a joyous shout and attacked it with fervor, but suddenly he gasped, spat it all out, and hurriedly gargled. The bacon, being pork, was of course forbidden to the followers of his faith. Looking abashed, he said, 'Sensei, please don't tell anyone of this.'

Nobody ever knew how this Egyptian earned his living. He would occasionally sell a huge slab of beef to the hotel kitchen; the next day there might be an article in the newspaper regarding the disappearance of a cow from the suburbs of Himeji, later found secretly slaughtered on the banks of the Kakogawa River. I suppose that Maged, working through some secret channel, acted as broker for such goods.

He was very poor, but he never pestered me for a loan. He must have been quite aware of my own poverty. While he was in the hospital I gave him fifty yen, but when he was released he gave it back to me, saying only, 'I am poor. Sensei is poor.'

Poor though he usually was, it occasionally happened that he came into sums of money that staggered my imagination. At such times he would suddenly turn into a sultan and release all his suppressed desires in one frenzied night. He would choose the youngest and most voluptuous woman from under our roof, even though he was ordinarily spurned because of his poverty, and invite himself to her bar. After showing off his wad of bills, he would spend the whole night with her at a hotel somewhere. The next day she would suddenly be rich. He would, once again, be poor.

All this was too much, and though it was out of character for me, I once advised him concerning his indiscretions. But he only gave me his usual wink, invoking the name of Omar Khayyam, the optimistic Persian poet, as though it were a magical spell, and even boasted of his conquest, saying something like, 'When Mariko drank water, I could see it moving down her transparent throat.'

I remember Maged telling me once that he had an uncle in Cairo who was a rich merchant, and that his prayer day and night to Allah went something like, 'May my uncle send a certain large sum of money to his nephew, whose circumstances force him to remain living in poverty in Japan.' According to my friend, the sum would be large enough to satisfy ten Marikos for about a year.

The route for remittance, he suggested, might be the International Red Cross or the Swiss Legion, or it might even be smuggled in on a German submarine. Of course it was nothing but a fantasy he returned to when he felt desperate. I sincerely wished it would come true, though, because the only pair of flannel trousers he owned had developed a hole in one knee, and he had cut them down into shorts. Now, in the extreme cold, he was reduced to warming himself in front of the heater in the hall. In spite of this, he remained barrel-chested, and where he shaved his face was as nice and blue as ever.

Maged was always spinning his tall tales. Those round-the-world chronicles were trail-blazing masterpieces of creativity, and however the stories were mixed they never bored me, no matter how long they were or how often I heard them. I never suggested that they might not be true. This Egyptian rogue claimed that during World War I he had been a sergeant in the Egyptian Army. To my surprise this turned out to be true. While wandering around the world he always kept a picture of himself dressed in an Egyptian military uniform, rather closely resembling those of the British, and sporting an upturned Kaiser moustache which he shaved off in later years. One day he presented this picture to me with his best wishes, calling me his best friend. His picture remains on my desk to this day.

Since that war in the desert, it was engraved in his mind that Germany was the enemy, so when the sailors from the German submarines drank beer in the hotel lobby, he would continuously throw conspiratorial glances at me. They always arrived with plenty of food and took away the women who lived in our hotel. No doubt, Maged saw them as formidable enemies. He despised the German sailors, criticizing the way their uniforms stuck to their bodies and their ridiculous bell-bottoms, and calling them toy soldiers. According to his theory, a proper soldier must be well built and reserved. Most of the Germans we saw were actually quite talkative.

I could easily observe the German sailors from my window. They would come up from the bottom of the hill in pairs, carrying in their arms food for an overnight leave on land, as well as (I swear I don't know how they got it) enough food for several other people. Even as they walked they talked continuously, face to face, and inside our hotel they behaved the same way. It was just a lobby, but they kept talking as usual. Their behavior must have been the same on the submarines. I had never realized that the Germans were such a talkative race, so it appalled me, and I was in full agreement with Maged's opinion of them.

He firmly held his tongue with regard to Japan's part in the war, but sometimes, and only to me, he would whisper, 'Japan is so pathetic.' This was his feeling even when the whole country was mad with joy over the great military gains made at that time.

Our hotel manager also liked Maged. This fine, grey-haired man was beloved by both the Japanese and foreigners, who all called him 'Papa-san.' He was the brother-in-law of the original hotel owner, whose wealth had been declining for some time, and the hotel had been sold. Because of his popularity, Papa-san was retained as manager, working late into the night as before, thanks to an ultimatum from the women residents, which had stated in effect, 'If Papa-san goes, we go too.'

Whenever the end of the month rolled around he went to great lengths to find innovative ways to charge Maged as little rent as possible. The manager's eldest son had already been killed in the war, leaving behind a young wife and baby. I often saw Papa-san and Maged sitting silently together in chairs beside the heater as if to comfort one another. The three of us enjoyed each other's company as we had many common interests.

Among the residents of our hotel, most of the Japanese depended on the hotel kitchen for their meals. Just keeping them all fed was a terrible ordeal for Papa-san. With such added strains, he died of a heart attack one night while sitting behind the front desk.

The women who gathered for his wake all cried, but the one who lamented most bitterly was Maged. He wailed and pressed his forehead against the soles of the dead man's feet. Was it because Maged was unable to return his friend's benevolence that he felt a need to receive Papa-san's blessing?

Two years later our wretched hotel was reduced to ashes. Now, nine years after the war, I have no idea what became of Mr. Maged Elba.

A WOMAN CALLED NAMIKO

Less than a month after settling into the strange hotel on Tor Road in Kobe, I spent the night with a certain woman, an event which eventually resulted in our living together for four years. I was unable to end the relationship even after the war, when Japan became an occupied country. Those four years did more to ruin my nerves than the war itself.

Though I am not a fatalist, it seems that citizens of nations at war acquire, little by little, a mysterious state of mind. When it comes to the matter of my first encounter with the woman called Namiko, I cannot but feel that she was dumped into my lap by somebody, or something.

But though I claim to have suffered, I had in fact escaped my past in Tokyo and must admit my good fortune at ending up living in the cosmopolitan atmosphere of the hotel in Kobe – unimaginable in wartime – actively searching for fresh experiences in a new life. My troubles after I met this woman must have been ones I invited upon myself. Having sown the seed of uncalled-for kindness one night, I was obliged to mow its weed-like troubles for the next four years.

In the winter of 1942 I was delighted by the prospect of living alone for the first time in my life. I was then a petty supplier of goods for a munitions manufacturer, but by that time there was such an extreme lack of products that I spent most of my day just listening to the high-flown fantasies of other brokers with as little to do as I. Almost every night I loitered about the cold harbor and drank cheap liquor.

After returning to the hotel on one of those nights, I chatted in the lobby with the Turkish-Tartars and the White Russian. We could not help but overhear the proprietress of some bar talking on the phone. She was saying such things as, 'Come back soon' and '*Ēsē yana.*' Since I didn't understand the meaning of the latter phrase, which was in dialect, I asked and was told that it meant, 'What good timing.'

After the call, the madam told us that three girls from Yokohama who were working at a bar in Kobe had been recruited by a larger establishment in Osaka, which in turn operated a bar serving as a brothel for military officers in Java. The girls had gone to the port of Ujina to take a ship to Java, but were stopped by the military police just before they boarded. The madam added that the reason for this would not be known until the three returned the next day, but in any case, the fact that they couldn't go was '*ēsē.*'

The next night I returned rather late to the hotel. Heading for the heater as usual, I found a woman already there. She was wearing an eye patch and cast stealthy glances at me. Though one of her eyes was concealed by the patch, her face seemed familiar. I ran through my memories of women's faces, and just as I finally remembered, 'Ah, that woman,' she said outright, 'Sensei, isn't it?' She called me this because she had been my patient when I was practicing as a dentist. She was from a brothel in the Honmoku district of Yokohama, but our relationship had never been that of prostitute and client.

At this point the story begins to take on a mysterious air. One day in 1938 I went to Yokohama with my friend, Watanabe Hakusen, the haiku poet, to visit our friend Higashi Kyōzō, also a haiku poet, who treated us to a large dinner of Nanking cuisine, as the local people liked to call it. I happened to discover that neither Hakusen nor Kyōzō knew what brothels were like, although Yokohama is known for them, so I introduced them to the one I frequented then.

Though I say introduced, it was just to drink beer. It was still early and the hall was empty, so Kyōzō told me that he had never danced in his whole life and he would like me to teach him. While the two of us were staggering around in the center of the polished dance floor, surrounded by mirrored walls, Hakusen, who had fallen asleep, chose that very moment to throw up a bellyful of Nanking cuisine. Kyōzō and I were terribly embarrassed, but a woman who had been leaning on the counter watching our clumsy dancing brought some newspapers and cleaned up after him, efficiently and without comment. As she turned to walk away, she said only, 'You ate *qingdou-xiaren*, didn't you?' It was certainly true, and Hakusen had eaten most of the stir-fried green peas and shrimp.

This quiet woman had been Namiko, who was to appear four years later wearing an eye patch – an almost magical coincidence.

Encountering a phantom from Tokyo just when I thought I had finally managed to escape made me feel ill. But I could never resist meddling, and so by asking her about the bandaged eye I unwarily contributed to the collapse of my cherished plans for a bachelor's life.

It turned out that the long-distance phone call of the night before had been from Namiko. She had left Yokohama for some reason and was working in Kobe, but wanting to get as far from Yokohama as possible, she had agreed to go to Java with her three friends. Unfortunately, one of them had been living with a foreign defendant in the espionage case against Richard Sorge, a German spy working for the Soviets, and the Yokohama MPs had been keeping her under surveillance. The women were prevented from boarding at Ujina at the last minute. Of course, Namiko was thought to be in suspicious company.

Namiko told me her eye had begun to hurt while she was staying at a boarding house in Ujina. When I questioned her more closely, she remembered that on the train between Kobe and Ujina, she had lent her handkerchief to her friend, who was complaining of irritated eyes.

Though it was midnight, I quickly placed a phone call to an eye specialist who was a relative of mine and forced Namiko to go with me in spite of her objections to how late it was. As I suspected, she had contracted an acute case of gonorrheal conjunctivitis and was told that if she did not apply medication to her eye every two hours throughout the night, she would lose her vision.

I took her to my room and treated her according to the doctor's instructions until dawn. Her eye was completely sunken and thick with pus. Was it because she had once cleaned up Hakusen's *qingdou-xiaren* that I took care of her all night? Was that the only reason?

Every two hours when I shook her awake, Namiko, tired and groggy, would say, 'Leave me alone.'

When I said, 'The doctor told me if I don't take care of you, you'll be blind by tomorrow morning, didn't he?' she only whispered, 'I don't want to feel indebted.'

These words surprised me terribly. I cannot say with confidence that I had no ulterior motive. Still, I was taken aback by her self-protectiveness at such a critical time. After all, she was threatened with the loss of her eyesight, so her suspicion that a man's kindness might bring her more serious trouble confounded me. Perhaps she was remembering past experiences.

When Namiko was living at the brothel, she seemed to be nothing more than a gentle and quiet girl, but in her heart she harbored a deep-seated distrust of men, and at this point in her life she had lost all hope.

It seems that she wanted to get as far away from Yokohama as possible because it was there that she had lost her first love. Her story was so similar to the plots of popular novels that it seemed rather weird to me. Her lover had been a talented young businessman. That he was still a virgin had also affected this prostitute's heart, and they had finally managed to live together after overcoming all kinds of obstacles.

But a popular novel must develop according to formula. True to the genre, his mother and a senior colleague tore them apart. The young man was transferred to a factory in Manchuria.

The following summer Namiko went there to visit him. She was not allowed to stay but, instead, was required to return to Japan and remain there while they waited for permission to marry. Desolate, she gave up her life at the brothel in Yokohama and took a job in a Chinese restaurant in the Ginza in Tokyo. (I actually recalled seeing her late one night on a train in Tokyo during that time.) While she was living in this unsettled situation, a letter arrived from Manchuria, saying only, 'Please give up. Nothing more is possible between us.' So typical, right to the end.

That same night Namiko threw a heartfelt curse over Yokohama, with all of its painful memories, and headed for Kobe.

Thus it happened that I, who had escaped the past by leaving Tokyo, and Namiko, who had run away from her memories of Yokohama, encountered one another again in the Kobe hotel. Having failed to escape to Java, her old feelings of despair were renewed, especially since she was now faced with having to repay an advance that she had already sent on to her natural mother in Yokohama. That night she must have had the urge to throw up something like *qingdou-xiaren* on me, a middle-aged man who cared for her all night long, but with a phony sort of kindness.

The next morning, the infection in her eye was much reduced, and within a few days she had completely recovered. But she remained angry with me for years over the unwanted kindness I had shown her that one night. For the next four years Namiko was to be a victim of my incessant meddling.

And that was not all. The cruel author of Namiko's life story was not content to release her with unrequited love. One year after she started living with me, we were lured to Yokohama by an urgent message sent through an aunt of her lover's, a woman who had been sympathetic to their situation. She told Namiko a story that almost made her faint. It turned out that the letter she had received from Manchuria, which had broken off their engagement, was one the young man had been forced to write by his senior colleague, and though he later wrote a retraction, it had been too late. Namiko had already left Yokohama for Kobe without leaving a trace. There were rumors that she had headed for Java. This melodramatic plot would have stretched the credulity of even the worst sort of novelist. After finding out about this, Namiko returned to Kobe looking like a lost soul, and about three times a day thereafter she would express a longing to go to Manchuria. What prevented her from doing so was the army, which had decided that nobody except military personnel could leave Japan. Even Namiko, who though appearing to be meek was in fact a very determined person, could not prevail against the sword.

For three years in the midst of the war and for a year after, I went on living with a prostitute whose heart was deeply scarred. My meddlesome but generous determination to protect her seemed rather depressing and ridiculous to a woman who, since childhood, had experienced more than her share of the world's bitterness. What she feared most was, in her own words, 'getting involved'; and she vowed never to begin loving me.

Often there were spells when we were lost in a reverie for days, and during such periods we would sense the merciless approach of the poverty that Namiko despised most. It was then that she would look to her friends, who were all working in bars and sleeping with the men they met there in order to earn enough money to survive. She could not possibly understand why I felt like tearing my hair out in frustration whenever she considered surviving in this way herself.

The reason she did not leave her officious middle-aged man was that she continued to hope that her lover might reappear, and she wanted me as proof that she had remained an amateur to the end. Whenever her survival instincts tempted her to return to old ways, I would threaten her by saying, 'I'll report this to Manchuria.' Then she would shrug her shoulders and stick out her tongue.

When her heart was not joyful, Namiko would round up all the kittens in the hotel and remove fleas from them one by one. While doing this, she would relate the history of her life in a slow, whispering tone of voice. As I listened to her day after day, I memorized every single story, but I would press her to tell me the same stories again and again. Whenever she reminisced about her lost childhood, she would dissolve herself in the past and, though it made her cry softly, her tears seemed to lessen the anxiety surrounding our precarious existence.

Her father had passed away when she was five, and she had been adopted by a farmer's family in Saitama, the prefecture just north of Tokyo. The adoptive father, being a gentle sort of man, sometimes combed her short hair for her, but his wife was an impetuous woman with a violent temper. This woman was confined to a mental hospital on occasion around the time Namiko was thirteen. The adoptive mother taught sewing to the neighborhood girls; the way she trained Namiko was quite severe, perhaps because the girl hated studying, preferring athletics instead. Namiko, who was usually so quiet when playing alone in the barn or shed, grew much more lively when taking part in sports.

One day when she was twelve, Namiko took her lunchbox and left for school as usual, but soon her attention was captured by a school of small fish in a rice paddy. She knelt at its edge and made a game out of trapping the small fish. Around noon she stretched her legs out on the footpath that ran between the paddies, had her lunch, and then filled her empty lunch pail with fish. Bent over on the footpath, completely absorbed in the amusement she had invented, she suddenly realized that beside her were two feet, and she had no idea how long they had been there. Badly frightened, she looked up slowly to find they belonged to her adoptive mother. At home she was punished by being confined to the barn, but her father kept going in to look for hoes, sickles, and so forth, which were not really needed, and as he left, he would pat her head or tug the braid hanging down her back. Once he left her two freshly baked sweet potatoes.

Namiko could never resist climbing trees though it was strictly forbidden by her adoptive mother, who often observed her from the window while teaching sewing class. No matter how quietly she climbed a tree, it grated on her mother's overtaxed nerves and she was soon discovered. The woman would appear beneath the tree, sewing quite forgotten, and poke Namiko from below with a pole from a clothes line. The girls would gather inside at the window and roar with laughter. Namiko hated those girls.

She loved to sing in her natural alto voice while sitting astride the ceramic gargoyle at the tip of the large tile roof. This quiet girl's tomboyish behavior continued even after puberty.

In the autumn of her sixteenth year, she saw a circus at the village festival for the first time and, determined to join the group, she drank vinegar every day in secret in the belief that it would make her thin. She chose a cattle barn for a gymnasium, and there diligently practiced standing on her hands with only a cow for her audience. One day, going around to the back of the circus tent, she asked a rather evil-looking man if they would take her with them. After inspecting her from head to toe, the man told her to come back at dawn the next day before the circus moved on with as much money as she could get and as many clothes as she could carry. That night after her parents were asleep, Namiko assembled a huge bundle of her belongings, but then she overslept as usual – which turned out to be fortunate as it prevented her from being sold off to a human trafficker. Her bundle of clothes was soon discovered by her mother, leading to her confinement in the barn for the whole day.

In the winter when she was sixteen, Namiko finally succeeded in running away. She went to Tokyo, and while walking along Dogenzaka Street in Shibuya, she saw an advertisement for a job posted at a cafe, and asked for a job there. It was plain to see that she was a runaway, and she was refused the job. Namiko, who was tenacious, spent the whole night sitting beside the frosty garbage can on the same street as the cafe, and the next morning asked again for the job. This time a policeman was summoned from a policebox nearby, and she was taken back to Saitama.

After that she made a habit of running away and was taken back several times, but at last she managed to land a live-in position at a cafe in Kamata, and at this point her parents gave up. At the cafe Namiko attracted the attention of a local gambler and eventually became his mistress, puffing on a pipe, with her hair done up in a butterfly coiffure. She was nineteen years old.

At some point her 'boss' lost a large wager, and forced Namiko into brothel life in order to repay the debt. He and her natural mother from Yokohama appeared every month at the hotel where she was living to collect money from her. Eventually the distorted pathways of her life had led her here to the hotel in Kobe, where she found herself picking fleas from kittens.

Four years later, after the war, Namiko climbed through the window of a train about to depart Sannomiya Station, which was the only way to board an overcrowded car, and, waving goodbye to me, went to visit her natural mother who had been evacuated to the countryside. According to rumor, she soon returned to Yokohama, married a black American soldier, and went away with him to America.

No one knows what became of the young man in Manchuria, but I imagine she gave him up for dead.

THE BRAVE SAILOR AND THE TAIWANESE

My two rooms in the hotel were upstairs facing out over Tor Road, which cuts right through town, sloping gently from the mountains down to the sea. At that time I was a businessman with little work to attend to. There were many days when I did not even show my face in the office I had taken in Kanō-chō. My occupation, if any, seemed to consist of gazing down, empty-hearted, at the passers-by from my window, holding my head in my hands and leaning my elbows on the red windowsill. Occasionally I would hear something like shouts of joy – voices raised by soldiers who were crowded into the trains crossing Tor Road at the bottom of the hill.

I was forty-five, and as I believe the upper age limit for military recruits was forty-two, there was no fear that I might be yanked into service. But among my haiku friends were many who were younger. One of them might be among the soldiers calling a joyful farewell to the citizens of Kobe from the passing train. But no, he would be sitting alone, behind his war buddies who were crowded into the window, shouting. Among my friends there was not one who would raise such a shout of joy.

After the suppression of intellectual freedom, which began with the Kyoto University Haiku Incident in 1940, we who were silenced by the government broke contact with one another. Once, though, a postcard came from Mitani Akira in Tokyo, saying that since he would soon be coming to Osaka to join a naval outfit based in Kure, he would visit me in Kobe.

Akira had been my close companion from the beginning of the New Rising Haiku movement, and he was with me during our time in the Kyoto jail. He had long suffered from tubercular arthritis, so I never thought he could be drafted. This young friend of mine not only had a wife but a child as well. Not until I received his postcard did I actually feel the looming presence of war.

Quite soon after the arrival of this postcard, he knocked

quietly on the door of my room. To my surprise, although he was going into the navy, he was wearing the khaki uniform of a common army soldier. Neatly attached was a red collar patch without a single star. I was overcome with pity and couldn't say a thing. He too had always been a quiet man, so that night, on our way to Osaka, we spent hours sitting across from one another in almost complete silence. During this time I could think only of his mother, who had died in a tuberculosis sanitarium, his younger sister, whose marriage prospects had been ruined, and his wife, who had come to Kyoto from Tokyo especially to bring him things while he was in prison. But of course I kept these thoughts to myself.

The appointed location for Akira's roll call was a dark, gloomy place under an elevated railway in Osaka Station. Notice boards had been set up with the names of the nearby prefectures. Before each board stood countless young men, and gathered around them were family and friends, holding the national flag in various sizes. Because it was almost completely dark in the wide area underneath the railway, people spoke with their faces pressed close together. The darkness was ominously swollen with the voices and energy emanating from the excited young men.

I was the only one who had come to Akira's send-off.

In time, the conscripts began filtering through the darkness and were absorbed into the station. The families and friends cried their farewells as loudly as they could. The khaki uniform of Mitani Akira the sailor soon vanished from sight. I wanted to shout something, but my voice caught in my throat.

After that I heard nothing at all from him, other than a report that he had indeed joined the navy. He was the only one of my friends I actually saw go off to war, so I began paying special attention to the naval reports. When the *Prince of Wales* and the *Repulse* were sunk at the same time, I felt like raising a toast to Akira and his navy, but I did not, having nothing around with which to toast them.

When I was a child I learned by heart a song called 'The

Brave Sailor.' Since there was a line in it that went 'Hasn't it sunk yet, Teien?' it must have been a song from the Sino-Japanese War. Until the war ended, every time I thought of Akira I whispered, 'Hasn't it sunk yet, Teien?' He had the serenity of a born hero, so I thought I knew what he would do at the moment of truth. But then again, the brave sailor might already be lying somewhere at the bottom of a tropical sea with many of his comrades. My sinister imagination grew more animated as the naval situation worsened daily: Akira lying on the seabed, clothed as he was when our friendship began, in a dark blue kimono splashed with white, wearing clogs with supports of magnolia wood ... or dressed as he was when I saw him last, in the uniform of an army recruit.

After the war he came to see me in Kobe, and it was then I learned he had never even left Kure. He had enjoyed a comfortable existence throughout the war as the highest ranking petty officer at the navy hospital there. When I heard that he usually had two or three slabs of *yokan* – a sweet which was practically unobtainable during the war – lying forgotten in a drawer, my mouth simply refused to close, and I felt I had been completely fooled.

Dating from the day I had parted from Mitani Akira in the darkness, even my hotel had become tinged with the shades of war as people from the foreign affairs section of the prefectural office and the plainclothes military police came and went incessantly. The hotel harbored a White Russian, Turkish-Tartars, an Egyptian, and others doing various jobs of a dubious nature. And as most of the other guests were madams, the hotel was thought to be a gathering place for unpatriotic folk.

Among such boarders as this, there was only one model 'Japanese': Keelung, a twenty-year-old Taiwanese, who lived in the room next to mine. Narrow strips of paper pasted on the window facing the road in his upstairs room formed the words 'Fight to the Death.' The letters were so huge that anyone glancing up from the road could not help but read them, even if he might not wish to. From morning to night, Keelung dressed in the national uniform, his legs tightly wrapped with gaiters. I, who possessed neither national uniform nor gaiters, watched his constant bustling activity in blank amazement.

He had come to be called Keelung because his grand ambition was to become mayor of the Taiwanese city of Keelung (rather than becoming the richest man in the country) – a novel idea, I should say, for the Taiwanese are skilled at making money.

He had a peerless devotion to tidiness. He scrubbed his room three times a day until it gleamed. Not content with polishing his own room, he would scrub my two rooms during his free time, clad in his national uniform and gaiters. Namiko and I would have to move from corner to corner to stay out of his way.

All of us secretly held this young man in high regard. Despite his desperate financial situation, he never tried to borrow money from the women in the hotel, nor did he drink or smoke. The main reason Keelung was trusted by the women was that he paid no attention to them.

During those days in Kobe, if a customer at a bar flashed a roll of banknotes and asked the madam to arrange for girls, it was understood they could never say 'No.' Once a woman had said 'No,' she would lose her job on the spot, and thereafter would find it impossible to get a job in any other bar, even if she wanted to, because the madams formed a tight community and word got around.

But these same madams were horrified at the thought of having men from the hotel where they lived visiting their bars. Needless to say, they were also against men taking any interest in women who stayed at the same hotel. All the women at our hotel were ruthless in their pursuit of men, yet they kept a sternly watchful eye on the Taiwanese youth and me. The situation did not affect me much as I was living with a woman, but Keelung turned into a little brother to all those women. Consequently, he felt he could not make advances to bar hostesses anywhere in Kobe even if he had wanted to.

Since the people in the neighborhood of our hotel were mostly Chinese and Taiwanese, the uproar during an air raid drill was quite bizarre. They could understand Japanese, of course, but were not so devoted to Japan that they would willingly obey Japanese commands. No matter that armbanded officials from city hall stamped their feet, no matter that they fell into a rage, ripping off their service caps ... whether in Mandarin or Shanghai dialect, in Fukienese or Cantonese, all Chinese laughter sounded the same.

At such times it was Keelung who carried the day. He became the self-proclaimed team leader, brandishing a homemade megaphone, carrying a ladder on his shoulders, climbing up onto the rooftops, slipping and falling into the water – such was the manner of his leadership. He would first give commands in Fukienese, then take the trouble to translate them into Mandarin, Cantonese, and the Shanghai dialect as well.

Since each room in the hotel was considered one unit in the neighborhood association, we lodgers were all expected to participate in each drill. But being just a bunch of unpatriotic folk, rather than rush to the drill we would get Keelung to be our representative while the rest of us piled up by the window in my room to watch the bucket brigade. After an air raid drill, Keelung would noisily scrub his room late into the night to express his anger over our lack of cooperation.

This exemplary youth was engaged in trade as a black marketeer. He traded in candies and dried bananas smuggled in from Taiwan. Every time a ship arrived, about five oil barrels of goods were carried into his room and sold to the women within half a day. They, in turn, would sell them to their customers in the bars for high prices.

As his business was progressing smoothly, with the approval of the women and myself, he decided to get married. His bride was a shop girl at a department store, and because of her respectability, the madams made a pet of her. Keelung became even more devoted to scrubbing.

His way of doing business was so audacious that he was finally caught by the Ikuta police. He refused to reveal his customers, but when his fiancée was questioned, she told them everything. Consequently, seven women from the hotel went marching majestically to the police station. Though they had learned of the confession from the bride herself, the seven women feigned complete ignorance in an effort to save Keelung. But hearing that his bride had confessed, he gave in at last, was quickly indicted, and handed a one-year prison term. Left behind, the young bride remained for a while under the patronage of the generous madams, but at last, unable to bear it any longer, she returned to her parents' home.

Since Keelung had given all his money to the hotel owner for safekeeping, I negotiated with the owner to ensure that Keelung's room would be held for another year. We would sometimes go down to the prison to bring him things.

Half a year later, Keelung escaped from the Kawasaki shipyard where he was working under guard. Suddenly our hotel became investigation headquarters, our lobby filled with prison guards, chin-strapped and tense, acting as though they all sought some important criminal.

We were told by the guards that, if captured, Keelung's sentence would be extended another year and that unless they could recapture him within twenty-four hours, by law the investigation would have to be turned over to the police. The madams gathered in my room feeling chagrined that the stupid young man had lacked the patience to wait out the year.

Keelung was discovered that very night hiding in the home of an old friend of his from Taiwan. Although he was surrounded by forty or fifty guards, he managed to slip away into the darkness by jumping from rooftop to rooftop. The women, who knew of his agility from the air-raid drills, were all smiles over their little brother's quick escape.

The next afternoon, with the twenty-four-hour time limit nearing expiration, the guards were becoming agitated, concerned for their personal honor before the regular police. At that point an old Chinese woman secretly called at my room. She told me that since Keelung was in hiding nearby, she wished me to retrieve the money that had been entrusted to the hotel owner instead of the bank. She handed me a piece of paper bearing the words, 'I beg you, Sensei.' It was obviously Keelung's own handwriting. Calling for the owner, I asked him to return the money and keep it a secret from the guards. This fat, swinish fellow, the ex-proprietor of a brothel in Yoshiwara, instead turned the old woman over to the wardens in order to keep the deposited money for himself.

Keelung, lying in wait nearby for the elderly woman, was chased down in no time by the pack of guards, who overwhelmed him in the restaurant district around the Hankyū Sannomiya Station.

The madams gathered in my room again to hurl abuse at the hotel owner, but it was like being a day late for a festival. Since I myself had acted as negotiator, it was painful for me to see them grieve.

Every time Namiko cleaned our rooms, she remembered the Taiwanese youth and condemned me for my clumsy handling of the situation. Though my excuse was reasonable, she insisted that I, with the title of Sensei, should have been able to think of some way to save Keelung. Her lack of understanding was hard on me.

By the time the war ended Keelung must have already been released from prison, but by then Namiko and I had moved further up the hillside, and in the postwar chaos I was unable to find him.

Directly after the end of the war there was a power struggle in Kobe between the Koreans and the Taiwanese. Gunshots were heard almost daily in the streets. One day I watched as an armored vehicle from the Occupation Army, machine guns stuttering, chased after a black limousine. At that time it was not the Japanese who were going around in cars.

The Koreans and the Taiwanese occupied the burnt-out buildings, hung up signboards for their organizations, and raised their flags on the rooftops. The Japanese only gazed up at them lethargically.

One day, as the armed struggle grew more and more intense, I was rambling around town on a bicycle with punctured tires. At one point several trucks appeared in my path, packed to the limit with people and displaying Taiwanese flags – a sun floating on a field of blue. As they approached, I could see that they were wearing iron helmets. Suddenly the man on the roof of the driver's cab of the first truck called out, 'Sensei!' It was Keelung. In a moment we had passed one another, but he turned around and waved with both hands for a long time. I got off my shabby bicycle and watched them recede in dumb surprise.

A few days later there was an article in the newspaper reporting a clash between the Koreans and the Taiwanese in which some Taiwanese were shot and killed. At the end of the article it mentioned that one of the Taiwanese, shot and dying, raised the cry of 'Banzai!'

That man must have been Keelung. At least I imagined so then.

BLACK BREAD AND DEATH

I believe it was in the spring of 1943 that the woman called Yōkō came to live at the hotel. As I have mentioned, more than half of its rooms were rented to monthly boarders – 'long-term residents' in hotel terminology. Plainly put, then, it was a boardinghouse, occupied for the most part by women, many of whom were madams who had served out their apprenticeships in the bars of Kobe. So when a woman appeared out of nowhere with only a suitcase and leaned on our front desk, I could not help but stop and gape, overcome with curiosity.

This was around the time when the war was still in its early stages. Women's clothing in town now consisted of baggy work pants, whereas every woman in our hotel still stubbornly wore slacks. Yōkō was wearing the standard cotton work pants and, although it was early spring, a dark, sooty blue overcoat. While talking to the elderly manager at the front desk, she cast her eyes about incessantly and raised her hand to touch her hair in unconscious confession of inner agitation. As I watched her, it occurred to me that the color and cut of her overcoat were familiar. It was the uniform of a Red Cross nurse. Somehow a nurse had strayed into this odd international hotel.

It is true that I felt curious about this woman, in part because I had worked in hospitals in the past and had developed an understanding of those who enter the nursing profession. But I admit that what caught my attention first was her arresting beauty. She was what is nowadays called *hattōshin*, or well-proportioned. Yet she was short and had a small face.

In that small face her eyes burned huge and black, with an intensity that took my breath away. Some time later when I was able to observe those eyes more closely, I found that their incredible shining blackness was due to the unusual length of her eyelashes. And the reason I say some time later is that, in spite of my expectation that she would be a one-night lodger, she took the cheapest room in the hotel and instead of staying for just a night, she became a long-term resident of the 'rubbish-heap.'

I am fond of the city of Kobe because the people here are open, and yet never interfere in one another's affairs. Despite the kind of life one leads, despite one's preferences, one enjoys personal freedom. This way of thinking fits my temperament. In the same way, the residents of the hotel showed respect for one another, and there was little occasion for any sort of malicious backstabbing. This changed when the nurse took up residence without a job. The other women began appearing at my door, one after another, spreading gossip about the Red Cross nurse.

The hearsay was, in short, that she had been working in mainland China as a nurse for the Red Cross but had been discharged when she became ill. Even though she had a brother in Shikoku, she chose not to return there for some private reason, and had come to our hotel after hearing that she would be able to survive there simply because she was a woman. I could not understand why the other women would be upset by this. When I finally said so, one of the madams, pouting, said that the last part of her story was unpardonable: 'Each of us works in a bar. We sleep with the military police even if they are harassing people. We bear it silently even when the foreign affairs people come to our bars without paying, yet' – gradually getting excited at the pathos of her own story – 'even though that Red Cross girl sleeps as late as we do, all she seems to do is spend her time in the lobby reading fortune-telling cards.'

Laughing in spite of myself, I replied, 'As long as a customer pays to stay here, I guess she doesn't have to work, does she?'

But the woman retorted, 'Men are so naive!' and told me that Yōkō admitted to the manager on her very first day in the hotel that she hadn't a cent to her name.

Hearing this, I thought, 'Oh no, here we go again.'

Once again, the burden had grown heavier for the gentle gray-haired old man. He was already carrying the responsibility for Maged Elba, who had no other home in the world, and every month was forced to new depths of resourcefulness in order to make his restaurant and hotel receipts balance in front of the hotel owner.

When I mentioned this, the women warned me that if this burden were added to those, our Papa-san's life span would be cut even shorter. This again brought to mind the swinish form of the hard-hearted owner.

Namiko not only agreed with every aspect of every opinion voiced by the madams but also added the absurd statement that she hated the idea of this nurse surviving by selling her body, amateur though she was. I sensed behind her words an intense hatred of her long life of prostitution and the circumstances that had driven her to it.

As for me, I did not want my room to become a conference center, so I reproached the women, for it was not like them to join in the persecution of such a pitiful lady. As I was speaking, their eyes flashed at me in unison.

'Sensei is on her side because she is beautiful. But we give our loyalty to Papa-san,' they exclaimed. Reacting to my words, their real distress was revealed at last. The woman called Yōko was so beautiful that the madams, who were severe in judging the looks of others, had become jealous.

In order to soothe the women, I promised to keep an eye on the Red Cross nurse and make sure she did not try to start any questionable business here at the hotel. At the same time I reasoned that Papa-san had guaranteed room and board to Yōko, even though she had no money, because his eldest son had been killed in the war on the continent, and he wanted to help a nurse returning from the same area. As it turned out, I was right.

As I mentioned before, the women at the hotel were fond of chatting in my room whenever the opportunity arose, but as spring passed in the blink of an eye and then the rainy season passed as quickly, I realized that Yōko was the only one who had never knocked on my door. Intuitively, Yōko may have sensed the deep-rooted antipathy Namiko bore her. Or she may have heard that I used to work in a hospital and felt reluctant to reveal her present circumstances. Or could it have been that she had had trouble with a doctor and was trying to avoid reminders? Running along this train of thought, my mind reached great depths of vulgarity, but I was still deeply disappointed that she chose to avoid me. However, I already had the odd, voluntary role of protector of Namiko, whose vows of chastity were none too strong, and so I had to content myself with furtive glances at the big black eyes burning in the lobby.

In Kobe there is a warm seasonal wind that blows from the west in summer, and so, unlike men everywhere else who are more properly attired, the men of Kobe go around in shorts and sandals. At night a cool wind blows in from the sea, and it is then that little groups of White Russians linger like shadows on the street corners uptown, talking on and on.

On one such night, I recognized two women standing there on a corner. They were Natasha, the Russian woman from the hotel, and Yōkō. As soon as they noticed me they averted their faces, but I could not have mistaken Yōkō's dress. It was so garish that it seemed to glow even in the dark. Blown by the wind coming up from the sea, it clung to her, revealing her slender outline.

I felt sick – she had gone into the business.

In the harbor at that time were German cruisers and submarines. With their escape routes under patrol by American submarines, they were trapped in the bay, where they remained anchored. With abundant food, and time weighing heavily on their hands, the sailors would steal canned goods and black bread from their ships and head for dry land to buy women. They could not fail to notice Yōkō, who was enough of an amateur to look timid but who nevertheless waited eagerly to sell herself. Although she had made this desperate decision, she still had a practical problem in that she didn't know enough German to succeed in the business. The German a nurse would know wasn't appropriate for striking a deal. This is where Natasha came in.

I had despised this forty-year-old woman, Natasha, from the first moment I saw her. Everything about her was offensive to me, from her wizened face with the deep red lipstick, and her sophisticated English and conniving Japanese, to the way she had of flicking her fingers while smoking. This middle-aged Russian woman acted as a pimp for Yōkō. Night after night the unlikely pair could be found standing together on the same street corner, staring in the direction of the dark sea, waiting for canned food and black bread. After striking a bargain with a sailor, the three of them would go to the hotel, and Yōkō would take him to her own room. Natasha would sit in the restaurant more often than not, and on one such night I found her sitting there alone, slowly spreading butter on black bread and removing sardines pressed in olive oil from a small tin. These she placed on the bread and ate smugly, her little finger raised.

From the direction of the room, I could hear Yōkō's cough, which seemed to be worsening. I attacked Natasha: 'Listen to that cough! It never stops. How can you sit here calmly eating black bread and sardines? That pitiful woman has a history that could have been written by your own Dostoevsky, yet you take her out every night and sell her to the German sailors you find on street corners. She means nothing to you but this black bread, which you sit and eat, oh, so slowly. You're like a bat, sucking blood from a victim who already suffers from consumption. Listen to her fierce coughing. And here you sit!'

The only answer I received from the Russian battle-ax was delivered in an English of almost sinister politeness. If she didn't help Yōkō to sell herself every night, she said, the girl would have to hang herself. Then she illustrated her point by coiling an imaginary rope around her own neck. She did this with a calm smile that I will never forget.

Saying only, 'Get her to a doctor!' I stalked back to my own room and said nothing of this to Namiko, whose usual line in any case was, 'Everyone can drop dead as far as I'm concerned.' Namiko would have considered the entire situation as a comedy.

The next evening I visited one of the other men in the hotel, the director of a hospital. We had never spoken before that night, but he was kind enough to come with me to Yōkō's room. Natasha was in there eating cake, so I drove her out first and then waited in the lobby to hear the doctor's opinion. He had been living alone in the hotel because he had sent his wife to a tuberculosis sanitarium in the mountains. The doctor soon returned and said, 'I give her about another month.' He also told me that the patient had been taking German cough medicine administered by Namiko. This shocked me, but I said nothing to her.

After talking it over with the elderly manager, we sent a telegram to Shikoku, but the only answer we received after five days was, 'I leave it to your discretion.'

The situation was so serious that the women in the hotel, who had previously shown the utmost antipathy toward Yōkō, now began to feel worried, more so because they had bullied her behind her back. Even though eggs were scarce in those days, boxes of them were delivered to Yōkō's room. One day all the women came to my room to tell me they wished her to be hospitalized at their own expense.

And that is how it came to be that Yōkō, through the hospital director's introduction, entered a hospital located about an hour from Kobe. I accompanied her there by car and twice had to administer cardiac injections into her alarmingly fragile arm. She no longer spoke a word, her eyes closed, her long lashes looking longer than ever.

She died ten days later, attended by the doctor on duty and a nurse doing the job that Yōkō herself had once done. The Egyptian, the old manager and I carried her to a crematorium and returned bearing a small urn containing her ashes.

From Shikoku we received word saying that in time someone would come to receive the urn, so could we take care of it until then. But since we could hardly keep such a thing at the hotel, we asked a temple to store it for us. A year passed, but no one ever came from Shikoku. Later, the temple was firebombed during the first air raid on Kobe. Thus Yōkō's ashes were burnt again, but this time without leaving a trace.

It was three years after her death that the word *panpan*, derived from the English word 'pom-pom,' was coined to describe the working girls who were found decorating the streets of our conquered land.

THE GO-BETWEEN

During the war, the inhabitants of our strange hotel judged one another's status on the basis of ration-book ownership. Yet even though she had a perfectly valid ration book, Harai-san remained a mystery to us, primarily due to her flat features, which unmistakably indicated her origin in continental China.

One of the madams, despite a policy of noninterference, was so suspicious of this woman that she went to the trouble of checking her ration book, which was on file at the front desk. It turned out that Harai-san was using her parents' address in Kawaguchi, Osaka. The madam was satisfied with checking back only as far as Kawaguchi, and thought to herself with the stupidity typical of her kind, 'She's Japanese after all.' In fact, since the Meiji era Kawaguchi has been a Chinese commercial district. Harai-san herself once told me she had an uncle there.

The reason the women stuck their noses into Harai-san's private matters, contrary to Kobe custom, was not only on account of her looks. It was her morality they questioned, which was lax even by the standards of Kobe's barmaids.

Harai-san led a perfect hand-to-mouth existence. During the day she slept soundly and ate nothing. At night she wandered among the bars she was acquainted with, doing temporary work. At that time, to say a woman was a barmaid in Kobe was the same as saying she was a prostitute. Harai-san would do business with anyone if it gave her a little pocket money. Of course, this was only in theory, since her flat Chinese face was not attractive to Japanese men. Since she spoke fluent German, her partners were often sailors from the German cruisers and submarines, all of whom were devoted to advancing her skills in the German language.

Her incredible ability to master foreign languages was not a typical Japanese trait. Of course the other women were jealous. For my part it seemed uncanny, almost eerie, to know that less than a year ago, when I first started living there, she had spoken only Italian in addition to her Japanese, yet now she could speak German fluently.

She had an unusual ability not only with foreign languages but with her own language as well. She spoke Japanese with upper-class intonations, which sounded quite strange in Kobe, where common speech was really quite crude. I know it irritated the madams that the licentious Harai-san spoke Japanese in a manner no less refined than that of the highest-born Ashiya women. I myself suspected that as a young girl she had been placed in domestic service with a sophisticated family somewhere between Osaka and Kobe. I felt sympathy for her in view of the hardships I imagined she must have endured from birth.

Women working in bars adopted nicknames such as Cheri or Mary, and called one another by these names all the time. But they were unwilling to acknowledge Harai-san by any name other than her own. For these women, Harai-san was mystifying and elusive, and they treated her with something approaching superstitious awe. Despite the degree to which she was held in contempt and fear, she remained absolutely aloof and quite insensitive to censure, having no qualms about calling at our room to ask, 'Namiko-san, is there a bowl of rice left?'

The war was becoming serious, and though the air raids had not yet begun, conditions in Kobe were beginning to change. Harai-san's freelance bar business was about to hit rock bottom, and upon waking in the evening she would begin to go door to door in the hotel begging for food.

About that time a friend of mine, an elderly German ship's captain, called on me in the company of an ugly old man with squinty eyes, and told me they had a favor to ask. It seems the old man wanted a bride. I listened to his story and learned that this ugly old German was a guard for a German naval supplies warehouse in Arima. He added that there was so much food in the warehouse that it would take even the voracious German sailors from the submarines and cruisers more than five years to eat it all.

As soon as I heard that, I thought immediately of Harai-san. Maybe this ugly old man wouldn't care about her flat face. As the proverb says, 'Even a broken pot can find a lid.'

So I went and roused her from her hungry slumber, forced her to make up her face, and took her to my room. There, with a table between them, the old, squinty-eyed German and the sleepy-eyed woman of uncertain nationality appraised each other. With him squinting and her still half asleep, as a matchmaker I felt quite uneasy.

The old man fell in love at first sight, but Harai-san was hesitant about making any kind of decision. I had forgotten that she was one of those people who sets uncommon store by good looks. So, in spite of the fact that she was practically a beggar, she showed absolutely no interest in the contents of the German navy's food stores.

Though I thought highly of her loyalty to her own ideals, I had a fair certainty that if she let this opportunity slip away, she would soon have to leave the hotel, maybe even tomorrow, and be reduced to foraging in trash cans. So I took her into the next room and, together with Namiko, urged her to compromise. She resisted, pouting with the cheeks of her flat face puffed out like balloons, but at length she yielded to our arguments and agreed to marry the warehouse in Arima.

Namiko and I were relieved to think that this would free Harai-san from having to go around asking, 'Is there a bowl of rice left?' for the remainder of the war, which could drag on indefinitely.

She reappeared the next day. She had about a dozen potatoes with her and a can of corned beef from South America wrapped up in a small cloth. 'Here, I'm back,' she announced indifferently. Like a spoiled child, she fretted aloud that she didn't like the ugly old German. I was unwilling to say, 'Look at your own face.' Instead, I persuaded her to reconsider, and got Namiko to accompany her back to Arima.

Even after that, Harai-san would reappear at the hotel almost every other day, carrying canned goods, humming a little tune, and flirting with good-looking sailors – behind my back since my presence made her uncomfortable. And as night follows day, the old German would rush into my room, his face crimson with jealousy, his breath poisonous, and give this meddlesome matchmaker a hard time. Thus it was that in less than a month the Japanese-German marriage was dissolved, and flat-faced Harai-san was back again in the same situation, complaining of hunger.

Although I had had enough of this business as a go-between for a barmaid, there appeared to be no end to my suffering. After Japan's surrender I once again became involved in the matter of Harai-san's marriage. By that time, in order to protect Namiko from the dangers of the air raids, I had rented a Western-style pile, which looked like a haunted house, further up the hillside. We were living in it when the hotel was reduced to cinders in the second air raid. Dodging incendiary bombs, Harai-san had made her way to our house after escaping from the hotel, and thus became a member of our family for the next six months.

Her second husband, after the war, was an American Army cook she had found by herself. As stubborn as she was, her hunger – which continued even after the war – had apparently exhausted her at last. One day she returned home and boldly presented me with a sort of certificate, typewritten and signed at the bottom by Pastor Somebody-or-other, and declared, 'This time I really got married, so please meet him.'

I gave her my hearty congratulations, pleased that her hunger would finally be over, but I was suspicious concerning the legality of the certificate. I didn't want to destroy the bliss which was apparent from the broad smile on her flat face, so I kept my suspicions to myself.

The next day she presented to me a small GI, about forty years of age, who belied her usual love of fair looks. The man had a face exactly like a monkey's. Apparently the reality of having lost the war had put an end to her taste.

The soldier had a sly look about him. He tried to persuade me that it was more than easy for an American soldier to get married, but gradually realized that I was tough to deal with, and by the time they left, his monkey face looked longer than it had been when he arrived.

Since Harai-san had complete faith in both the pastor and the certificate, she moved out of my house and took a room, welcoming the monkey, who visited her there as her husband.

I thought it all right if her hunger was over once and for all, and she was happy. But one day during a visit from an American officer who was a friend of mine, I showed him the certificate that I had been safekeeping and, as I had suspected, it turned out to be counterfeit. The officer flew into a rage and told me he would bring the matter before the military tribunal.

It took great effort to calm him down. He had answered the call to arms when he was still a student, and from his point of view, any American soldier who deceived a miserable Japanese girl and kept her as a free whore brought shame to his country. Yet from my point of view, if the monkey were brought to trial on criminal charges, Harai-san's own history would come to light, and worst of all, she would go hungry again. In my own home there was no food at all, and we were at a complete loss as to how to cook the bran, distributed as emergency rations, in order to make it edible.

Of course, I hated the monkey-faced soldier. I then learned that men like him are referred to as 'smart alecks' in American slang, but no matter which officer or soldier I asked for a proper translation of this term, I was never satisfied with the answer. In any case, I kept it a secret from Harai-san that the certificate was a fake. My heart ached over the whole matter, but the pain was eased by the American. That is to say, the man to whom Harai-san was supposedly married left the army one day and returned to his country without a word to her.

Another woman would have cried in shame and anger, but Harai-san possessed a unique moral outlook, and there was none of this. She stayed quite calm, saying only, 'To hell with the monkey!' Her command of American English had made great strides during her 'marriage.' After that she became a housemaid and temporary wife to an American lieutenant commander. They would often come to visit us in a huge car.

I wonder how she's doing now. Could she be dozing all day again in order to forget her hunger?

Very often I become disgusted with myself for my tirelessly meddlesome ways. Looking back to my hotel days, I remember yet another case when I served as a go-between.

In the alleyway next to the hotel there lived two brothers named Won, from Canton. The eldest was about sixty years old, the other around fifty. Both lived in a two-room den that was too filthy for words.

The younger Won was a chair repairman, and I made his acquaintance on a balmy autumn day while I was repairing a bicycle tire, which seemed to get punctured daily. I must have looked like some kind of engineer to him, since he asked me to repair a light in his house which had been broken for as long as ten days.

This was the first time I had been in their haunt and I was stunned by the extreme filth and gloom of the place. I soon discovered the only thing wrong with the light was that the fuse had burnt out, so their single bulb was soon working again.

After that, the younger Won's estimation of me was rather larger than life. He began bringing me every imaginable sort of problem. For example, even though he was Cantonese, he was a believer in St. Daishi. Every year in early spring until the beginning of the war, he would go on a pilgrimage through all eighty-eight Buddhist temples in Shikoku, following in the steps of the saint. But after the war began he could not make his pilgrimage without proper permits. He tearfully begged me to do something about this, showing me a tattered Osaka newspaper clipping about his pilgrimages through Shikoku, seeming to believe that because I was called 'sensei,' I could do anything.

Saying 'I have money,' he pulled a bundle of hundred-yen notes from his grimy waistband. He anguished over the situation, worried that he would suffer the wrath of god for such long neglect. I told him that if anyone were to be punished it would be the foreign affairs section, who forced him to stay here, and that the matter should not cause him such distress. He said nothing but only rustled out his pilgrim costume with its many red seals, and wore it to show me how it looked. I thought his strong belief was admirable, but I did not have the courage to brave the foreign affairs section on his behalf. I couldn't live up to his confidence in me, though it was touching.

And yet, being unable to give up, he would often badger me about the pilgrimage. One day he called on me, offering an unidentified slab of red meat wrapped in bamboo leaves, and abruptly asked me to find him a bride. He told me that he had once met a woman who had also been on a pilgrimage alone to the temples of Shikoku at the same time as he. They had married and returned to Kobe together, but after two years she had died.

'Since she must have been a gift from St. Daishi,' he said, 'I treasured her to the fullest. Find me another such bride, please.' He made this request as though he thought I already had one in my palm. Even after that, he was convinced I could provide him with another bride, and he would remind me about it impatiently. I was completely at a loss, and finally became disturbed to the point where his face appeared three times its normal size in my mind.

While working overseas in my youth I had been treated kindly by Cantonese people. Though it was impossible for me to do as good a job for him as St. Daishi had done, I decided that I would have to find a suitable woman to console him in his old age.

At that time I was a businessman dealing with a munitions company. I had an office, which was filled the entire day with a lounging crew of famished, devil-like brokers. Choosing from amongst them, I picked one who seemed comparatively accommodating and confided Mr. Won's wishes to acquire a bride. He immediately accepted the responsibility for finding him one, and to my surprise brought a woman to the office the very next day.

The prospective bride was a little over forty, and had a strangely elusive expression. The broker explained that she had been widowed, and that she was a decent sort of woman who was employed at a workshop for the disabled somewhere. As I watched the bride-to-be's simpering face during this explanation, I had a rather uncanny feeling about her character. Her intellectual capacity, too, seemed doubtful. Nevertheless, once again I became a go-between, and I led her to Won's hovel.

Mr. Won was brimming over with rapture. That very same day he found a neat, clean room and moved in, and from the next day onward he beat a fan drum every morning. I found it hard to believe that such a devout adherent of St. Daishi would really be beating a fan drum, so I went to the trouble of calling at their new home to find out for myself. It turned out that his new bride was a follower of the Hokke sect, which beats the fan drum. The virtuous Mr. Won had aligned himself with her beliefs, but he confided that, while they beat the drum together, he uttered the chant of his own sect.

This same Mr. Won took great care of me after the war. At the time of the conversion of the yen, he went to the bank on my behalf and deposited my old, worthless banknotes. Beginning the next day, and every day thereafter, he would return to the same bank teller's window, demanding, 'Give my money back! Give my money back!' The bank finally gave in to his persistence and provided him with updated banknotes, which he then returned to me.

I heard later that Mr. Won's wife had gone insane from beating the fan drum too fervently, and had eventually died.

THE GERMAN SHEPHERD

The day was quickly approaching when Kobe would be destroyed by air raids. I was sure of it even at the time. Though I had no intention of waiting helplessly, I knew of no countryside location where Namiko and I could move for safety. I thought I could at least rent a room somewhat higher on the hillside as a refuge, so I searched out a place on Yamamoto Street. I paid six months' rent and yet remained living in the hotel, being strangely attached to this nest of quirky people. Namiko continued picking fleas from the collection of hotel cats, and I continued supplying goods, although not very many, to munitions companies, while buying food from the German sailors. In this way I lived from day to day, making a scanty living with no future.

In the summer of 1943 I finally decided it was time to leave the hotel. On that day I received a visit from a Danish friend named Beck, who had been an engineer on a Danish ship. After his last ship left he had settled in Kobe, and lived with his Japanese wife, who was known as Mary at the bar where she worked. The four of us had gone swimming in Maiko. Returning to the hotel all tired out from the exercise, Beck and I went to the public bath behind the hotel to wash away the salt water.

Mary was accustomed to calling her husband Beck-chan, and so we followed suit, although the man easily stood taller than six feet and '-chan' was a diminutive more appropriate for a young child. Here in the crowded public bath he stood quite at ease, pouring hot water over his body again and again with composure, but because of his size he did not go into the water to soak.

The patrons of the bath were, of course, people from the neighborhood, and of the twenty or thirty who were there only a few were Japanese. A fat Chinese man, a Taiwanese, and a Cossack who resembled Taras Bulba chattered away, the babble of their different languages echoing in the narrow space. All of these foreigners, stark naked as they were, retained a stately poise, even though the day was drawing near when a rain of incendiary bombs would fall from above them. Among them, only the Japanese seemed timid, hiding their fronts self-consciously with their towels. Watching these happy, fatalistic people in the public bath, I came to the realization that, when the time came to save ourselves from the fire bombs, not one of them would lift a finger.

We left the hotel the very next day and moved into the house on the hillside. It had been built for foreigners in the first year of the Meiji era, and by now the paint was crumbling and the floor creaked. The rooms were cavernous, twenty-tatami spaces that gave one a feeling of emptiness.

A young painter and his family had been living in the house, but soon after we moved in he was drafted and moved into a factory residence. I bought their few bits of furniture, and we became the sole residents of the house.

Some time after the war, this spooky, European-style house came to be called Sanki Mansion. I do not know who named it, but most likely it was one of the following writers who had visited me there: Mitani Akira, Ishibashi Tatsunosuke, Higashi Kyōzō (now known by the name Akimoto Fujio), Ishida Hakyō, Yamamoto Kenkichi, Nagata Kōi, Andō Tsuguo, Enomoto Fuyuichirō, Hirahata Seitō, Hashimoto Takako, Suzuki Murio, Sawaki Kin'ichi, or perhaps someone else.

As my neighbors had done, I tore up the flower garden and planted vegetables. I fertilized the garden by opening the iron lid of a septic tank and dipping out the turbid water that drained from the flush toilets in the homes of the Russian Vashikov and the Frenchman Blume. I also dug a large air-raid shelter beneath the garden.

There in the dilapidated house, in a room like the main hall of a temple, Namiko and I lived quietly day and night, exchanging few words.

Besides Namiko, my family consisted of a dog, a cat, two canaries, a pigeon, and a bagworm moth. The bagworm was a special autumn guest. While we sat silently facing one another, our shadows looming large on the adjacent wall, it would appear at the edge of our huge table and crawl slowly across the surface, dragging its shelter behind it. It did this for about a month until I finally returned it to a nearby acacia tree.

The cat was one of those that Namiko had been keeping at the hotel. This cat would use the tin-roof eaves for a toilet and pretend to cover the results with soil.

The canary had been kept inside a German submarine to test air quality, and while we were keeping it at the hotel, another flew in from somewhere, attracted by the singing. They became a pair, so we bought them a cage.

The pigeon had been with us practically since its birth, when someone had given us one of two chicks. When its downy feathers gradually appeared, it no longer enjoyed being caged and, instead, was set free to amuse itself in the room. While I was tilling the field, it would fly out and perch on my head, pecking at me as if to say, 'Keep still!' as I swung my hoe. After the war American soldiers walking along the street would stop and ask me to sell them the pigeon. As though it understood English, the pigeon would fly away at top speed toward our house.

As I had been expecting, very soon after we moved into Sanki Mansion, Kobe was turned into a field of cinders by two air raids. But our haunted house remained untouched.

The hotel, as I had predicted, was instantly reduced to ashes by a shower of incendiary bombs. Only the storehouse was spared, though the heat killed about a dozen cats the hotel owner had locked up there before he fled. These cats were located in a heap just inside the door.

The madams, who escaped the flaming hotel with only the personal possessions they could carry, all rushed in a panic to Sanki Mansion. Once again, it seemed, I was living in the strange hotel.

What saved us all from starving were the potatoes, which I had grown with my own blistered hands, and the occasional chickens Maged would find somewhere, which we roasted whole.

I also had to find milk to feed the baby of one of the refugees, who had been so terrified during the air raids that her milk had stopped. Of course, in the ruined city it was all but impossible to find such a thing as powdered milk. In the end it was Mr. Won, the Chinese chair repairman, who saved the baby.

I ran into him amid the burnt-out ruins. Though he listened to his former matchmaker without comment, that same evening he brought a Chinese woman whose breasts were about to burst. She had been discovered by Mr. Won, holding her swollen breasts and crying over her baby, which had been killed in the air raid. After this, she came to the house several times a day to nurse the refugee's baby, and always left in tears.

Among the women who had escaped the hotel was a big-boned woman named Naomi, who had been born on the Korean peninsula. Ever since the day she began living at the hotel, she had tried to keep her heritage a secret. I became aware of it, though, because in Sanki Mansion she slept in the room next to mine and talked in her sleep during the wee hours of the morning, very distinctly in Korean. I was not the only one who heard her. Some of her other friends from the hotel knew also, but none of us ever mentioned it to her.

Most of the refugees at Sanki Mansion found suitable accommodations within a month or two, but Naomi and two or three others remained with us for much longer.

On the day the end of the war was announced on the radio, Naomi was the only one among the residents in my house who cried for Japan. Listening to the Emperor's voice, she wept bitterly. My aged French neighbor, Mr. Blume, who had been living in Japan for thirty years, also shed silent tears as I told him the content of the broadcast. I felt a bit ashamed for being unable to cry as Naomi and Mr. Blume had. Later, as I considered the nature of the old Frenchman's tears, it occurred to me that he may not have been weeping over the defeat of Japan at all. As for Namiko, she had never shed tears of sadness before, and this time she could only retch in her misery.

Naomi had a lover named Otto, who was a cook on a German submarine. He and other German sailors and officers had been staying at the Hotel Rokko during the war and continued doing so after the German defeat. However, their treatment there changed radically, in keeping with the international situation.

In the beginning, when the Germans were prevented from leaving Japan because of the Allied blockade, they were treated as special guests of the Japanese Navy and accorded the privileges of allies. After the defeat of Germany they became, in effect, the captives of their former protectors, and after the defeat of Japan, their position was reversed yet again, in that they became captives of the American military. Through all of this, the men remained in residence at the Hotel Rokko.

The American Occupation army seems to have behaved with some generosity toward the German sailors. Often around nine in the evening, Otto and his friends would walk down from Mt. Rokko to Sanki Mansion, a distance of some kilometers, stay up past midnight dining with Naomi, and not return to the Hotel Rokko until the next day. I was amazed at the vitality of these people, but at the same time they reminded me of dogs in heat.

When it was decided that Germany would be divided, the American forces became even more generous with the Germans. Naomi finally rented a cottage on Mt. Rokko and started living with Otto. Besides Naomi, some other Japanese women were also invited by their lovers to settle on the mountain.

Buildings were already being requisitioned from amongst the ruins of Kobe. A so-called 'comfort facility' for American military personnel appeared, where hundreds of Japanese women could be found day or night, working or dining. I was the head of the liaison section of a construction company after the war and had many opportunities to enter such places quite freely.

Naomi and the others on Mt. Rokko, however, did not try to earn dollars by coming down from the mountain. There were rumors that the German soldiers were to be sent back to their country soon, and these women, destitute as they were, clutched their impoverished German men and despised those making a living at the foot of the mountain. It turned out that the women on the mountain were receiving nothing tangible from the German soldiers. Not only that, these women would go down to the city with clothing they had managed to salvage from the flames, sell it at a high price to the prostitutes who were dealing with black soldiers of the occupation forces, buy American cigarettes as souvenirs, and go home to their men on the mountain.

I received an invitation to visit Otto and Carl one day and, ascending the mountain path, I saw one of the Japanese women, Maya, taking a walk with her lover, a former German officer whose legs had been blown off during an air raid in Kobe. She was pushing him along in a wheelchair. I was reminded of a play I had seen in the old days, and I stopped to reminisce, watching them until they were out of sight at a bend in the path. I am sure that neither Maya nor her lover had ever heard of such a play.

Otto was keeping a huge German shepherd. I had seen many dogs in my day but never such a huge dog as Otto's. This dog survived on plentiful table scraps from Hotel Rokko, and now stood here in dazzling splendor, reflecting the summer sun on the mountain. Naomi doted on that dog so much that Otto was frequently jealous.

In time, rumor became fact, and the German soldiers were gathered in Yokohama for the trip home. It was decided that the Italians would also be repatriated. To my surprise, several Japanese women departed with them to Germany and Italy. What surprised me even more was the 'generosity' of the American Army for allowing this. At the time, it was suspected to be some subtle policy of collusion among white men.

Naomi lived on Mt. Rokko for about two months after Otto and the others had left, remaining there with the huge dog. Otto had told the desperate woman to sell the dog in order to make a little money to survive, but she refused to exchange the reminder of her lover for money. Descending the mountain, she would come to visit me, but would soon begin to fidget and would finally return home, explaining that the dog would be getting hungry.

In the end Naomi came down from the mountain and sold the dog for ten thousand yen to a Taiwanese man, but I only heard this story from Namiko much later.

Naomi moved from Mt. Rokko, and did not appear at my house again for some time. One unusually chilly evening I saw her standing behind a telephone pole in front of the Daimaru department store in Moto-machi. As I came nearer, I could see that she was crying, sobbing as at the time of the Emperor's broadcast. When she recognized me, she seemed to relax a little, but even so the tears would not stop for a while. When I asked what the matter was, she told me that Otto's dog had just passed by in a car, and when the German shepherd saw her, he had tried to jump through the closed window.

Though it was just a tale of the thwarted reunion between a dog and its master, so ordinary as to be trite even to me, yet I understood that to Naomi the dog was the incarnation of the German sailor, Otto.

There was nothing I could say to comfort her, but she was glad enough to come with me anyway. So we climbed the hill above the cold city, returning to Sanki Mansion, the run-down house once built for foreigners.

JOURNEY BY CAR

Let me now return to a time before the air raids. While I was living at the hotel, two or three gentlemen took the trouble to visit me from time to time from out of town. These men, already emotionally drained by the desperate state of the country, would arrive completely exhausted by the long train ride. And yet, seeking my company was not the only purpose for their coming, I imagine. Born believers in freedom, despite the increasing lack of it around them, these men seemed to come all this way drawn by my descriptions of the bizarre, cartoonish life at the hotel.

Of these visitors, the one who traveled farthest and consequently took the biggest trouble to reach my quirky place of abode was Mr. Shirai from Tokyo. And this prematurely gray-haired forty-year-old man was the only person who had nothing to do with haiku.

Mr. Shirai was the eldest son of a shipping agent in Tokyo's Tsukiji. He developed a love of adventure when he was a child, and this grew over time. In the Taishō era, he went to France, where, with some difficulty, he eventually become an airplane pilot. Then at the outbreak of the First World War, he served as an officer in the French Air Force and fought alongside Baron Shigeno. At that time in Japan there were only a few pilots who were not military personnel, so his life could have been a rather glamorous one after returning home following the war. However, in reality, it wasn't. He never held a regular job because he couldn't bear the constraints of being an employee of a company, as he had a natural inclination for adventure and a spirit that embraced freedom.

I met this vagabond adventurer in 1941. We both had the same strong antipathy toward government authorities, but most of all we despised the swine called the military.

We were also two cosmopolitan, good-for-nothing human beings who couldn't believe in the value of a stable life, or in having to yield to the necessary obligations of that kind of existence.

We found it impossible, in fact, to call ourselves family men: it would be dishonest and hypocritical. In short, we were kindred spirits. We quickly became close friends.

Shirai's first visit to the hotel was in the middle of the summer of 1943, and of course it was accomplished in his characteristic style. He drove from Tokyo to Kobe.

I was puzzled. For one who had no real occupation whatsoever, I thought it could hardly be possible that he owned a car. Moreover, at a time when a popular slogan proclaimed, 'Every drop of gas is equal to a drop of blood,' he arrived with as many as ten cans of gasoline. I was more than surprised. I was completely dumbfounded.

He was wearing an open-necked shirt, an alpine hat, shorts, and tennis shoes. He drank a glass of water in my room and then, saying there was not much time, asked me to please ride with him as far as Maiko. He then told me that his ultimate destination was Hakata, Kyushu. This, once again, surprised me. I got into the car as he urged and, sitting next to him in the front seat, listened to the rest of the story. It turned out that the car had been borrowed from the army by the aviation section at the Asahi newspaper in Tokyo, and he had volunteered to return it to Kyushu for them.

Before the war, Shirai had been associated with a private automobile club and a motorboat club, among others, and was a regular speed demon. So he had grabbed this rare opportunity to dart out of Tokyo for his first extended road trip in a long while.

We passed by Maiko in a blink.

'A bit further,' he said, 'as far as Himeji.'

We passed Himeji in a blink.

'Let's go a bit further,' he said. 'Let's eat something good at this town far from the railway. I'll let you return from Okayama, so let's eat together in the fishing village called Katakami tonight.' As he spoke, he drove faster.

Resigning myself to fate, I settled back in the speeding car, which had little army flags fluttering from the hood.

Flying dizzily along the narrow ribbon of Japanese coastline at top speed in a military car with military gasoline and no purpose other than to deliver the car were two middle-aged men, both of whom hated both the war and the military, racing further and further westward under a flaming sky.

Our first overnight stay was in Katakami village in Okayama prefecture. We ate a bit of fish and drank a bit of saké. Fearing that the fishermen might steal the gasoline loaded on the car seats, we took hourly turns patrolling the area, and consequently had a rather miserable time.

I had been determined to return home by train from Okayama, but the next day we went straight through the city, far to the south of the station. Having driven through, Shirai showed me maps of Okayama, Yamaguchi, and Fukuoka prefectures for the first time and told me that it had been his intention all along to kidnap me in Kobe and take me with him all the way to Hakata.

It was much too late to insist that he let me out of the car. For one thing, I had no money to return by train, and for another, I was exhausted. I surrendered to the inevitable and closed my eyes for a little rest.

By this time, I was amazed by the sheer physical energy of this ex-French Air Force officer. He could not chance dozing off in the car. If he did, we would overturn, the gas cans would ignite, and we would end up as human torches. So he never dozed but drove at full speed along the country roads under the flaming sky, not even taking a drop of water. I was the only one doing any drinking.

'If I drink any water, I'll get tired,' he said. 'So I'd better not.' When he felt hungry, Shirai crunched noisily on stale bread.

I was not so unrealistic as to expect a comfortable trip by car during the war, but while tearing full-tilt like a wild horse through the silence of the scorched land and munching on stale bread, I had the sudden conviction that both the driver and passenger had been born in the wrong time.

Our second overnight stay was in the city of Iwakuni. We ate a grand dinner, but even while eating, the thought of having to guard the gasoline all night weighed so heavily on my mind that the salt-grilled *ayu* fish, which I hadn't had in years, tasted no better than sawdust.

The next day was the same: flaming sky, wild horse, water in a canteen, and stale bread. Since it was impossible to get a decent map like the ones drawn by General Staff Headquarters, all we had was the rough kind one can buy at train stations. As a result, we were getting lost with terrible frequency. Whenever we got lost, it was the job of the navigator, namely me, to ask for directions. In addition to the hunger and lack of sleep, I felt irritable and so did not ask for directions properly. Consequently, we got doubly lost. Shirai eventually became irritable also, and accused me of being a lousy navigator.

A narrow river flowed through the mountains along the road in Yamaguchi prefecture, and in front of each and every house there was a twenty-gallon barrel with 'Fire Prevention Water' written on the side, right there next to the river. We passed through other small villages, the mountains rising steeply behind them. All had watchtowers as tall as fire lookout posts, yet they stood at the foot of mountains so high that if one climbed them, one would command a view of the entire Inland Sea.

That evening we crossed by ferry from Shimonoseki to Kyushu and, taking off again like a mad horse as soon as we landed, we arrived in Hakata around eight.

Shirai broke into a broad grin and said, 'Thanks a lot for all your trouble.'

With a resigned air I, too, tried to smile, but all I managed was a twitch around the lips.

Half a year later, just as it began sleeting one evening, Shirai again visited the hotel in Kobe. This time, he said, he had flown as far as Nagoya in a plane owned by the newspaper company, and then had had to stand the rest of the way in a train. One of the reasons he had come was to see me; the other was that I had told him during the trip to Hakata that the old manager of the quirky rubbish-heap hotel in Kobe had graduated from the same elementary school in Tsukiji, Tokyo, as he had. He was extremely eager to meet him.

There was one more reason, perhaps the most important. Though his close-cropped hair was a premature, snowy white, forty-five-year-old Shirai, glowing with youth, had heard my tales of the hotel and wanted to revive memories of his past in Montparnasse. For this reason he had braved a flight by Cessna through frigid skies, his teeth chattering, and down below had stood the whole way on a train, as if bound for hell.

I thought it rare that two childhood friends should encounter one another after so many years, but I did not really think it exceptional. The reason I say this is that I myself had had a similar experience once. One day in 1941 I had sold some junk to a secondhand dealer in Tokyo. Among the stuff was a certain wall hanging which had been used in a Javanese play. Three years later I came across the same hanging at a secondhand toy corner in the Hankyu department store in Osaka. There is no such thing as fate in Japan; the place is just so small that these things are bound to happen.

However, this meeting between two gentlemen could not really be considered commonplace under the circumstances. It was wartime, and they had been reunited by me, their mutual friend. The moment had its drama, though more on the scale of a puppet theater than the grand stage.

I asked Papa-san to choose a woman for my old bachelor friend, who needed to recover from the fatigue of his journey. It was not Shirai's request, though. Being a true-born Tokyoite, he was particularly proud. Despite his body pulsing with hormones, he was a man who never confessed his needs.

So Papa-san and I discussed our mutual friend in whispers and made up a list of requirements, which turned out to be rather strict: she must be good-natured, non-professional, young, tall (Shirai was a tall man), and most of all, she must be beautiful.

Today, these conditions might serve to select Miss Japan, but such a woman did actually exist in the room next to Keelung's, whose room was next to mine. Yes, she certainly existed, but how could we make such an impolite request? She had once worked in a coffee shop, and began to lodge at the hotel only because she had so many brothers and sisters still at home. Hoping to better herself, she was currently serving an apprenticeship for a career as a projectionist. I had to weigh the benefits of helping a friend from afar against the hazards of tempting a young woman to transform a temporary dalliance into a permanent occupation. I voiced my concern about this.

The old manager suggested, 'Let me ask her.'

That is how it happened that our white-haired friend warmed his frozen body that night.

I had doubted that she, unlike any of the other women under this roof, would accept such an indecent proposition. At the time I was teaching her English, in spite of the government injunction against it, and found her polite and intelligent, as well as beautiful, just as our conditions required. I confess that upon hearing of her acceptance of the temporary post of concubine to Shirai, I felt a gust of cold wind blow through my heart. It was clearly a disappointment for me at the time. My heart ached at the cruelty of lotus petals scattered in the mud.

Nevertheless, there had always been some question as to how she managed to live in the hotel on so little capital. It was revealed later that the reason the manager was able to ask her this favor without great anxiety was that she had already offered to grant such a request, under the provision that the man was a gentleman. Shirai was not the first such gentleman. My concern for this fallen lotus was unfounded, yet my disappointment stayed with me forever.

Shirai appeared the next morning looking as though a weight of darkness had been lifted from him by more than just the passage of night. This free-spirited man, who had neither a wife nor children, was so taken with the young woman that he made her a gift of every penny he had with him, through the intermediary of the manager. She put it all in the bank and went cheerfully off to her job as an apprentice projectionist.

From that time on Shirai would often appear out of the sky, bearing gifts of dried vegetables, canned goods, dried rice cakes, and such to present to the young woman, very much in the manner of older unmarried men. She would diligently carry these rations to her younger siblings at home. Though their poor house was in the alley right below the hotel, the younger children were strictly forbidden to visit their sister there.

The madams under the same roof protected her. That is to say, they pretended not to notice how she lived. I, too, decided to overlook her kind reception each time Shirai flew in. I told him as much. That is why I continued to teach her English as usual right up until the day I moved out of the hotel.

Anticipating that air raids were imminent, I moved further up the hillside. Before long, my prediction proved right. The whole city of Kobe was devastated by the second air raid, and the hotel was reduced to smoking cinders. The first question I asked of a maid from the hotel who had managed to escape to my new abode was for news of my English student's safety. The maid told me that the young woman had rushed out of the hotel and down the road to her family's house as soon as the air raid alarm began to blare. I set off immediately toward their house, running through the burning city, leaping repeatedly over fallen electrical wires.

The vacant lot in front of her alley had been given over to build a bowl-shaped fire-prevention pond. Along the concrete edge of this pond the bodies of the drowned were already being laid side by side.

Racing along the streets on my way to her house, I had seen many charred bodies, but here the sight of the drowned, who bore no burns even in this scorched neighborhood, was a sight too cruel and tragic to witness. Fearing the worst, I continued to search. At last, circling the pond's edge, I recognized a familiar summer shirt on one of the drowned. She was lying with her little brother still clutching tightly to her right arm. On her left arm hung the old secondhand bag that Namiko had given her. Seeing this with my own eyes, I could only turn and run back the way I had come as fast as possible. On the way I stopped only once, overcome with a violent attack of nausea. I could not escape the memory of the wild lamentations of the survivors around the pool.

Since the war ended, I have heard nothing from Shirai.

Perhaps these two, who loved one another without regard to their difference in age, are now together somewhere, speeding down the single straight road of the afterworld in a car.

I wonder if they have cars there....

THE NIGHT-BLIND GENTLEMAN

I have mentioned Mr. Shirai, who visited me at my rubbish-heap hotel, but my Kobe story would be too tame if I did not also invite a another gentleman, Mr. Wada Hensuirō, to step into these pages.

Our friendship dates back to around 1937, the year he burst onto the haiku scene at Kyoto University with his first literary criticism. It all started on the day the editor of *Kyōdai Haiku*, Hirahata Seitō, received from an unknown writer a critical essay entitled 'A Quest for Seishi's Poetics.' It was signed by Wada Hensuirō. From the very beginning, the Kyōdai Haiku group had included a large number of intellectuals, unusual even among haiku groups in the New Rising Haiku movement, and consequently criticism was flourishing. This unknown critic's work, a frontal assault upon a titan called Seishi, who at the time seemed to have the power to knock flying birds from the sky, created quite a sensation. Seitō even thought that Wada Hensuirō was the pseudonym of some famous haiku poet. Moreover, the handwriting in the manuscript bore a strange resemblance to that of Hino Sōjō, who was considered Seishi's chief rival, and both Sojō and Seishi were affiliated with Kyōdai Haiku as well.

The editor must have been pretty excited, but by the time the text was in print, it was discovered that the author was a newspaper journalist who had graduated from Kyoto University. He was immediately invited to become a member of Kyōdai Haiku. In the face of this new challenge, which had appeared like a shooting star from such an unexpected source, Seishi himself took up his pen for a rebuttal entitled 'A Work Without a Map,' in which he wrote, 'Mr. Hensuirō, bearing the family name of Wada ...' From the sound of that, it seems Seishi remained convinced that Hensuirō was a pseudonym.

In this way Hensuirō made his dramatic entrance into the world of haiku. His passion was for literature, of which haiku is but a deformed child, and his brief enchantment with this genre was dampened by the foul rice that he, along with his haiku friends, was forced to eat in prison during the intellectual oppression of 1940. He left the world of haiku after that.

While I was still living in Tokyo, I exchanged long letters with Hensuirō, who was living in Osaka. After I escaped from Tokyo and came to Kobe in the winter of 1942, our friendship flourished. I had no other friends, and I often visited him at the newspaper offices where he worked. He visited me in Kobe as well. If our friendship seemed to deepen rapidly, it was because we were invaluable to one another as confidantes. We had no one else to turn to who could understand the almost inexpressible anguish we endured in those days. Neither his wife nor Namiko had any interest whatsoever in our literary discussions, yet they often felt some jealousy over the intimacy we shared. They would listen to our disputes without comprehension, but, even so, when I lost Namiko hated him, and when he lost his wife hated me, which amused the two of us. Hensuirō and I passed the time this way in pointless debate – such silliness made it easier to bear the weight of the gathering storm and the uncertainty of ever seeing better times.

Now it is said that I am a kind man, but Hensuirō's kindness was of a greater magnitude, and so it usually happened that it was I who was in his debt.

At the beginning of the war, Hensuirō was in charge of press coverage for the railway industry. Whenever I could afford a round-trip ticket between Kobe and Osaka, I would visit him in the building owned by the railroad. In the restaurant there, we could get coffee and sugar such as we never saw a hint of anywhere else. Hensuirō, who had no sense of taste, would get talking and absentmindedly keep adding sugar to his coffee. When I would stand up to leave, it became my habit to glance into his coffee cup. There, at the bottom, I would invariably find at least two spoonfuls of sugar melted into a pool of syrup.

As I have often mentioned, business was terribly slack due to lack of goods, and the day had long since passed when I could hope to double my money on a load of secondhand bathtubs. With money becoming so scarce, Namiko's fidelity was constantly challenged. Which is why I went to Osaka with a parcel wrapped in cloth, led Hensuirō out of his office, and persuaded him to take me to a pawnbroker. He told me there was a municipal pawnshop that had a very low interest rate. At the window of the pawnshop he boldly presented his business card, pretending it was a news-gathering visit, and then, just as we were leaving, he whipped out my parcel. It was clear that the prestige of the card with his company name would prevent the forfeiture of my possessions.

So in the blink of an eye, most of my clothing became the temporary property of the city of Osaka. When even that seemed unlikely to be enough to protect Namiko, I would wrest a watch from Hensuirō's wrist or plunder his camera and make him take me back to the pawnshop. No matter what time of day I appeared, he never failed to welcome me. As though it were his duty to help me keep Namiko from falling from grace again, I took every advantage of his good nature.

During the war, the cold winters were terribly hard on the malnourished people of Japan. One snowy day it happened that I had to visit a certain fishing village near Sasebo where I kept my love child. I had only enough money for a sack of potatoes, which would have to serve me for several meals. Naturally I decided to visit Hensuirō and see if I could borrow his rail pass, good for travel on all routes. There was never any end to his kindness, but at the same time he was a rather timid person.

First of all, he gave me no fewer than ten business cards, complete with company name, telling me that when a conductor becomes suspicious he always asks for a business card, so to show not one but several at a time. Next he checked my suit. Finding a small tag with my name on it, he removed it with a knife. At the station to see me off, he told me to be careful at least a hundred times. I am none too bold myself, actually, and was reluctant to travel so far using someone else's pass, but still I felt his misgivings were excessive as I boarded the frigid, second-class train.

Unfortunately, the second-class train was full. Since I was riding for free there seemed no point in complaining, so I took a seat in the waiting room at the end of the dining car. At the same time, another man entered and sat down beside me. It was incredibly cold in there, and of course there was no radiator. Hensuirō was very kind, but not to the extent of sending me off with saké, so I was shivering all over when the gentleman next to me turned and remarked, 'In this cold it seems likely that if one were to fall asleep, he would surely catch a cold. Though it may be a bother to you, let's try and talk while we travel. How far are you going? ... Oh, the same as me.'

When he said this, I was greatly distressed, knowing that before long I would have to exchange business cards with him. Since the man was not a conductor, it would have been all right to tell him my true name, but a conductor would come along sooner or later and then I would be bound to offend my traveling companion by handing out a different card with Hensuirō's name on it. All these things I had to consider while I sat there shivering. He knew nothing of this, naturally, and handed me his card. Taking the situation as I found it, I handed him one of the cards belonging to Hensuirō. As would be my luck, he said that his company was located near the newspaper office, and that he also happened to have many friends on the staff there.

'What section are you in? ... Is that so! Then you are with Mr. So-and-so. His wife and mine are friends, and we often make a foursome ...'

I anticipated over ten hours of this torture, sitting with icy feet and a fiery head, and wondered if I should confess the whole thing after all. Hensuirō hadn't thought to brief me on his company's circumstances, so here I was, a poor middle-aged man who was only here in the first place because he had made a foolish mistake in the past. You should never have a love child.

Later, returning to Osaka to give back the pass, I told Hensuirō of the ordeal on the train, and he insisted that we go see the man together. To prove he wasn't kidding, he took the business card the man had given me and telephoned him on the spot. The man was not in his office, and to this day, more than a decade later, I still don't know exactly why Hensuirō was so interested in meeting him. If I had to interpret his actions, I would say that his curiosity was of a literary bent.

In 1943, B-29s often appeared over Tokyo, but in Kobe there existed a strange nonchalance, an easy optimism characteristic of international cities. Under the influence of this mood, I rambled about in a kind of fog, vaguely wondering what to do with myself. I got into the habit of taking a fishing boat out of Maiko whenever extra money rolled in. When Hensuirō heard about this, he was struck by my nonchalance and asked me to take them with me by all means, 'them' being Hensuirō and his friend Mr. Kotani.

After the war, Kotani appeared as the main character in 'Bullfight' and some other stories by Inoue Yasushi. He was portrayed as an enterprising and enthusiastic, though melancholy, newspaper journalist. Until the stories were written, I had not known Kotani was that kind of man.

One summer night, Hensuirō appeared at my hotel in the company of the short and almost femininely gentle Kotani, though we were not to go fishing until the next day. I suspected they had come the night before because Hensuirō had told stories about the strange residents of the hotel, and they wanted to do a little on-the-spot research. Not only were they skeptical, they were newspaper reporters.

Unfortunately, nothing of true literary quality occurred at the hotel that night to satisfy their expectations, aside from a late visit from Mary. She was terribly drunk and carried a huge handbag stuffed with banknotes, which she tossed into my room for safekeeping. Taking advantage of the opportunity, she rushed in after it, wearing nothing but her chemise, and hugged me from behind, coaxing me into singing the lullaby from the French opera *Jocelyn*.

At Maiko the next day, we hired a boat with a skipper and went fishing, but the only fish I caught were some ugly things called *tonkochi*, which have huge heads and almost no flesh. Hensuirō had different luck, but no better, for while the fish he caught were the beautiful, five-colored *bera*, they are almost completely flavorless. These were just about the only kinds of fish anyone ever caught in the area, but Hensuirō was still tickled by it, declaring, 'Sanki catches the rogues, but I catch the princesses.'

We both felt a bit sorry for the hero of Inoue's future story, who had not managed to become acquainted with either princesses or rogues.

The skipper seemed to feel equally sorry for all of us, and suggested that we try catching octopus for a change. He produced a colander containing a coiled length of fishing line with a small, narrow board attached to one end. A cuttlebone and an amaryllis bulb painted with coal tar were bound to the board, and a lead weight and a large hook were attached to its edge. According to the skipper, by tossing out the bait and dragging it across the sea floor, octopi that like coal tar and amaryllis bulbs could be lured to swim up and wrap their arms around it.

We were very impressed by the wisdom of the man who had discovered the preferences of the octopus, and we each took a baited board, swung them over our heads, and threw them into the sea. In spite of the skipper's advice, Hensuirō did not bother to coil the tip of the fishing line around his finger. As a result, he lost the whole thing: hook, line, and sinker vanished into the sea without trace, all for some octopus to hug, leaving only the colander in the hand of a skeptic. The skipper looked as though he wanted to cry.

Despite our attempts, nothing we did amounted to a real diversion, and we headed back to shore with our usual solemn faces. On the beach, Kotani, who had been rejected by all sorts of fish, had the only luck of the day in the form of a platinum Waltham wristwatch, which he discovered in the sand – a rather large catch. Unfortunately, a neighborhood fisherman, upon hearing of our discovery, appeared and claimed the watch, saying it had been lost the day before by one of his customers. He hurried away with it, leaving Kotani with nothing more than a feeling of gloom.

Hensuirō was a tall fellow, nearly six feet, and had a robust appetite. Since sugar was the only abundant food at the railway house, and as he was quite picky about what he ate, Hensuirō soon became night-blind due to malnutrition. If his height had been normal, he would not have gotten into such a pathetic state.

One autumn day he surprised me by appearing in Kobe, aimlessly wandering about, his hair cropped almost to nothing. This timid, hairless giant had come to visit me in the house on the hill overlooking Kobe, where I had just started living. I bedeviled him as usual with an ironic discourse on the virtues of women, but Hensuirō the ladies' man, unable to bear my sarcasm, refuted my opinions with a serious expression. Since this was wartime Japan, we also focused our attention on more current issues. On this day our conversation shifted towards the training of soldiers with exceptional night vision, similar to that of owls, enabling them to operate effectively at night. For a man suffering from night blindness, this subject was rather depressing as well.

Soon evening fell. Hensuirō decided to take a bath, so he went to the one just outside the kitchen. Next to the door of the bathroom was the door to the stairs leading to the back room upstairs, which was occupied by the teacher of a sewing school.

She was already a war widow, but since our house was closer to her school, she lived here instead of at her own home. On that day her mother-in-law, worried about her living conditions, had come to see for herself. Arriving in the gathering twilight, she stood quietly, looking for the back door of the large house.

I did not know she was there, of course. At the time I was sitting at the table with Namiko watching a few of our pet bagworm moths crawling on the table, lost in reverie, which was abruptly shattered by the sound of a great shriek from outside.

Rushing to find out what was the matter, I discovered a white-haired woman pressed against the wooden wall of the bathhouse, wide-eyed and shaking with terror. It seems that the door right in front of her had opened and a stark naked bald man, six feet tall, had emerged with arms outstretched in order to avoid bumping into any obstacles, which his pitiful, night-blind eyes were unable to detect. He was as startled as she, and could only stand there in confusion, calling out my name again and again.

Nowadays, fashionably dressed, Panama hat and all, the once night-blind eyes never fail to spot even the slimmest outline of a figure approaching from as far as a block away. With an exclamation of, 'Look at that one!' he rushes ahead, forgetting his companions.

After the war, this timid ladies' man became quite forward with women in response to my encouragement. His sudden boldness has caused many problems, which he brings to me to set right.

What a long and muddy road!

PARBOILING SHARK

I have already written eight chapters and will continue yet a while, but to tell the truth, I wonder why I am writing these stories. If my only purpose were to amuse my readers, it would be better to write pure fiction instead of enumerating actual events with such obstinate loyalty. My purpose would seem to be not simply entertainment. Could it be that I write for a publication fee? No, I regret to say that the money I receive for each chapter of *Kobe* is hardly enough to inspire me to stay up all night.

Little by little I have grown to understand that my writing has but one purpose, which is to reveal the stupidity of one being, known as Saitō Sanki. That is why these tales seem not to be written for anyone but myself. Though they may cause me dishonor in the eyes of future generations, I desire to expose the full extent of my witlessness, which can strike at the worst of all possible moments.

Being aware of this makes me suspicious of memoirs. I trust neither Wilde nor Rousseau, nor even Akutagawa Ryūnosuke, as far as their confessions are concerned, though I believe I understand their motive for writing, perhaps better than anyone else.

In the very first chapter I admitted coming to Kobe to escape everything I had ever known in Tokyo. The main reason for leaving was my anger over the extent of my own stupidity – not over any specific act of wrongdoing, but because of my incomprehensible foolishness. Ever since childhood this aspect of my nature had become more obvious to me. Now, having reached forty, I am finally resigning myself to the likelihood that my life will know no end of it.

One example of this is that I allowed a woman to persuade me to give her a child.

We had first met in 1934, in Tokyo, and though we eventually became more than casual acquaintants, I already had a wife and child, and so never anticipated having another child, regardless of who the potential mother could have been.

Around that time, in the autumn of 1935, I developed a serious case of a pulmonary illness, but I soon entered a state of remission. However, in the spring of 1938, I fell seriously ill once again and had to be confined to a hospital, where I remained in critical condition. During that time, this woman, who worked by day in another hospital, nursed me, often throughout the night. This woman – well, maybe I should stop referring to her in such a remote and standoffish manner (she might get angry with me) – is named Kinuyo, and in fact I can hear her this very moment chopping something in the kitchen.

Kinuyo's parents, who lived in a house on the seashore near Nagasaki, had grieved over their eldest daughter remaining in Tokyo. She had not responded to their suggestions of marriage, though her marriageable age had nearly passed.

By 1939 I had miraculously recovered my health. I quit dentistry, started working for a company, and opened my own business as well. Having once gazed into the unfathomable abyss of death, whenever I closed my eyes its image returned to me. What had saved me was the unlikely combination of a doctor heavily addicted to narcotics, and a nurse named Kinuyo.

Before dawn on the last day of August 1940, I was led from my home by a police escort and was detained for some time thereafter in Kyoto. Kinuyo, who had selected me as a partner owing to her overly kind disposition, embarked upon a rather imprudent undertaking. Immediately after my arrest, she began to submit one written petition after another to the marshal of the Matsubara police station, where I was being held. I was completely dumbfounded by this, but not as surprised as the marshal, who already had enough trouble handling this annoying Sanki person who had been dumped on him by the secret police. It was to him that Kinuyo's letters were addressed, one after another, each attempting to persuade him, based on her experience, that the man under detention was a morally upright individual quite incapable of any wrongdoing or the plotting of evil deeds.

It was an annoyance and a vexation, but the marshal never failed to take these letters to the office of the secret police. Once he tossed them at me while I was eating a sweet bean jam bun, looking as if he wished to say something. But as it was unclear what kind of criminal I was, he would hesitate and walk away across the creaking floor. By the way, the bean jam bun was something found with great difficulty by the petitioner, who had to search all over Tokyo to locate such a rare treat.

I was released that same autumn and returned from Kyoto. It was in the spring of the year after next, 1942, that Kinuyo approached me with a difficult request. She wanted to have a baby.

When I asked in astonishment why she wanted a child, she explained that her elderly and hard-working mother in Kyushu had fallen ill with uterine cancer. Feeling she would not live much longer, the mother had pressed her unmarried daughter for a grandchild. Kinuyo was by nature and upbringing a dutiful child, and wanted to fulfill her mother's wish while she was still alive. She was afraid, however, that her mother would be gone by the time she found a husband. And even if she could manage to find a husband so quickly, she was not at all confident of being able to give birth to a child in time. So she desperately begged me to help her have a child before her mother died. Being a nurse, she was fairly sure that her mother would not last more than a year. As she pleaded with me, I could see she was quite distraught.

My life had been saved by this woman, who had nursed me while I lay at death's door. I had been uncertain whether an opportunity would ever arise to repay this debt, but now it lay before me. If the only way I could repay her was by acting as a stud in order to please both her and her dying mother, I could hardly refuse, even though I had doubts about the ultimate success of the project. If a baby were born, he would have to be hidden away. I thought that perhaps, after he had grown up, he would learn to understand that he had been intentionally conceived, and that he might then forgive me.

A fool thinks vaguely in this manner.

Spring passed into summer, by which time Kinuyo was certain she was pregnant. Life preceded death! I do not know just what sort of letter Kinuyo wrote home to her parents, but she heard back from her father, who asked her to return home promptly with her bridegroom. But her 'bridegroom' was forty-three, someone else's husband, and already a father.

I have since given considerable thought to Kinuyo's motives. Was it only because of her mother that Kinuyo so desired to have a baby? Is it not also likely that by giving birth to my child, she felt she could lay claim to me and challenge any rival for my love? Fool that I was, I thought only of my debt to her, and blamed myself for having been persuaded by the circumstances. By co-operating with a request made by someone I could not deny, I found myself in immediate trouble, which continues to this day.

Anyway, at that time I received the astonishing news that I would have to travel all the way to Nagasaki in my role as the bridegroom. Exerting the full strength of my oratorical powers, I tried to persuade her of the unacceptability of this idea. But being pregnant gave her a certain self-confidence, and she remained convinced that she would bring her 'bridegroom' with her. At other times, her confidence would evaporate and she would weep, pulling me down to earth like a punctured balloon.

You may have heard the sayings, 'Sink or swim' and 'In for a penny, in for a pound.' In China there is an expression, *mei fa zi*, which means 'It can't be helped.'

In the autumn of 1942, then, I found myself sitting in a train bound for Kyushu, lost in reverie. Next to me, Kinuyo, her belly swollen, praised the scenery passing outside the window, her face a picture of great satisfaction. For her it was a bride's first call at her parents' home. She was even carrying the baby her mother had been awaiting with such anticipation.

My face was reflected in the window. I stared at it without

being able to tear my eyes away. The mouth moved, saying something. In rhythm with the echoing wheels of the train, it mumbled, 'I've never heard such a story.'

We decided to take a night's rest at Moji. Having asked for directions from the tourist bureau at the station, we soon arrived at a drab and filthy inn. Inside there was a charcoal brazier with chopsticks stuck upright in the ashes. The meals were to be cooked by the travelers themselves, and though it was already chilly, there was no warm food. There were no tongs, either, so there was no choice but to use the chopsticks from the ashes to pick up the thickly battered sardine tempura, and to warm it over the poor fire in the brazier, which I coaxed to life by blowing on it. While eating the stale tempura, that voice again whispered in my ear, 'I've never heard such a story.'

The next afternoon we arrived at Kinuyo's home, a house overlooking Ōmura Bay, the waters of which were as still as a lake. The scenery was the sweetest in the world, but for someone in my situation, what is the good of scenery?

I performed a formal bow by kneeling in front of her parents with my palms on the floor. What I said is now forgotten, but perhaps I said nothing at all. I remained in this position for quite a while, during which time I thought, 'This is strange. This has happened to me before.'

And so it had. Being no ordinary fool, I had already had the experience of posing as someone's fiancé, and finding myself in the same circumstances again, the memory was returning with uncomfortable clarity.

I had been twenty-six at the time, soon after my life as a student had finally drawn to a close. Though my marriage to a long-time fiancée was near at hand, and we had already made arrangements to go abroad in the winter of the same year, I suddenly fell in love with a newspaper reporter. From that summer into the autumn, I spent every day and night feeling like some insanely revolving lantern.

In those days, female journalists were extremely rare, even in Tokyo. The reason no one suspected her of scandalous behavior, in spite of her beauty, was that, blessed with wisdom, she placed great importance on her work and pretended to have no interest in men.

She, too, had an elderly mother who did nothing but wait for her daughter to present her with a fiancé. This is where I stepped into the picture.

In spite of being a 'modern girl,' a popular term then and one I have always disliked, she thought very highly of her mother.

Knowing that the date of my marriage was set for November, and that there was absolutely no way in the world I could escape it at the last minute, she asked me 'for mercy's sake' to see her mother and pretend to be her future husband. 'Please help answer her long-awaited wish, no matter how terrible a lie it is.'

I actually considered attempting double suicide with her, but instead I did quite a noble job of acting like a proper fiancé in front of her mother, thinking that it was one of those once-in-a-lifetime situations.

The exhausted youth had no way of knowing that he would reenact the same scene twenty years later in faraway Kyushu, making a thousand silent apologies during a long, drawn-out bow to another elderly mother. What hell life can be!

Kinuyo's aged parents welcomed me to the shore of Ōmura Bay with an artless sincerity and in a heavy dialect I could hardly understand. What I did understand was that they loved their daughter, who had chosen to live in Tokyo, and they wished to pay all due respect to the middle-aged man she had brought to meet them.

The day after we arrived, the father treated the half-hearted bridegroom to fresh octopus, which could be caught in the sea just below the garden. I tried groping under a rock for an octopus while standing knee-deep in seawater, but all I got for my efforts was a crick in my back. The older man would now and then straighten up and tap the small of his back.

Kinuyo, speaking easily in a dialect I could hardly understand, reminisced with her parents, carried forage to the cow shed, cut vegetables in front of the hen house, and did other chores. Watching her as she did these things with such natural skill, I was impressed. She did not seem to feel that she was deceiving her parents in any way. Her goal was to present them with a child, to deliver it as soon as possible, and it was certainly no lie that the child inside her did exist. But this was the part that I, as a man, found the most difficult to understand.

The next day was the one I dreaded the most: the day of the banquet in honor of the new couple, to which all the relatives had been invited. On that day, the house was inundated with visitors right from the early morning. In the kitchen were neighborhood women shouting at one another in that dialect which sounded like a foreign language to me. In time, the men returned from the fish market. The fish were to be carved by those gathered for the engagement banquet, in keeping with local custom.

As for me, sitting on a seaside cliff in the company of a lot of sea lice, I closed my eyes and resigned myself to fate. When curiosity got the better of me, I peeked from behind the backs of the men to see what kind of fish they were preparing. What I saw were two gray sharks lying limply on the ground, each no less than three feet long.

Soon boiling water was brought, and the sinister-looking fish were turned over and over while the boiling water was poured over them to loosen the skin. After that, one of the men laid a piece of wood on the ground as a cutting board. The rough gray skin was stripped away with a thick sound, exposing the meat, which had the same disgusting grayish color as white catfish.

The man who had removed the skins also separated the fish into three chunks and began vigorously slicing them into sashimi. I felt nauseated, and so I slipped away to squat in front of the chicken house. But somehow the rough sharkskin, hacked into irregular lumps, had preceded me there and was lying in the feeder. There seemed to be no escape. My face must have been the same color as the skinned shark.

Kinuyo's elderly mother smiled at me graciously and invited me to take a bath. In the bath house, whose walls were straw instead of clay, I obediently removed my clothing. In order to save water and fuel, the water was only knee-deep. Squatting on the tiny wooden platform, only about two feet in diameter, I once again closed my eyes.

The banquet lasted from noon to night.

The shark sashimi was piled in great heaps on huge dishes, to be dipped in vinegared miso and devoured by one and all, irrespective of age or sex, while simultaneously carrying on frantically animated conversations. The plate was passed many times to me, but in order to avoid throwing up I stubbornly kept my eyes closed. As for the saké, it was so bad I could not force it down.

In time, these good citizens of the seashore began to sing a song with a sluggish sort of tempo, clapping in time to the music. I could not understand all the words, but the general idea, appropriate to the occasion, was something along the lines of: 'There's the sun, there's the sea, fish and shells, a man is strong, a woman is fruitful....' Or so it seemed.

Kinuyo was giving me furtive glances. I clapped my hands along with the others in time to the music, and while my plate was right in front of me, piled high with food, a cold sweat beaded my forehead due to my hunger.

My jacket was drenched with saké spilt by people who had good-naturedly urged me to drink. Before long, the cold liquid had seeped through the lined kimono I had borrowed from her old father, making my knees clammy and cold. Without quite knowing when it began, I realized that I was shivering uncontrollably.

It was under these trying circumstances that I first began to feel something akin to love for the unborn child within the the woman who sat beside me. That night I did not leave the banquet until it was over, although I continued to shiver.

The following day I was sick, suffering from chills, vomiting, and diarrhea until I finally fainted. I knew I could not possibly have been poisoned by the shark I had refused to eat, so the cause of my illness must have been those pearl oysters which lay in the sea at the back of the house.

Looking down from the garden, the sea was only four feet below, and further down on the bottom, four or five feet below the surface, the big shells lay everywhere. When I asked Kinuyo the day before if they were edible, she said that although their harvest was prohibited in this season, the flesh was thick, and when broiled, they were 'yummy!'

'If they're yummy, let's try some.' Speaking these few words in the local dialect, the groom had roasted them on the brazier and had a bite for lunch, thinking all the while, 'This is sure to disagree with me.'

Ten minutes later, as I had feared, I was writhing in agony. I was told that no family member had ever been ill from eating them. It could only have been the judgment of Heaven on me for being such a fool.

The next day I left for Tokyo alone, leaving Kinuyo for an extended family visit. Kinuyo's mother died the following year, having seen the face of her grandchild.

It was in the winter of the same year of my return from Kyushu that I escaped from Tokyo. Though I say from Tokyo, it was in actual fact the 'fool in Tokyo' from whom I so wanted to escape. I finally acknowledged this hard truth when I became disgusted with my foolish behavior, which resumed as soon as I arrived in Kobe. It was at that point that I began to realize I could not escape, no matter how far I went to get away from myself.

> Fleeing – yet
> the fierce afternoon sun stalks
> the defeated cock

It was after the war that I wrote this sketchy haiku in Banshū.

Kinuyo is now my wife and the child she begged of me is a freshman at a junior high school.

THE CAT-CRAZY CUCKOLD

As I've mentioned before, the owner of the hotel was quite large and round, bearing a resemblance to a well-fed swine. After making a small fortune in Tokyo by methods I will elaborate on later, he bought a cheap hotel in the middle of Kobe, which was close to his hometown, and making only a down payment, moved in with his family. I happened to move in at almost the same time.

I had worked in a British colony when I was young, so I felt quite at home, both among foreigners of sundry national origins and with the hotel's tough bar hostesses. I never felt out of my depth.

In contrast, the new owner was unable to get used to the atmosphere, even when he sat by the warm heater in the corner of the lobby, and could only stare at the faces of the people staying in his own hotel. His unbelievably tiny eyes, buried in his large, fleshy face, roamed about nervously. This behavior stemmed partly from his inability to understand foreign languages. Furthermore, conversation among the women in this cosmopolitan city differed from standard Japanese.

All the residents of the hotel, men and women alike, vigorously resisted the unparalleled form of violence known as war. The common attitude among them was based on the idea of 'Freedom to Us.' Which is why the Egyptian, the Turkish-Tartar, the White Russian, the Korean, the Taiwanese, and the Japanese women living in this dump could be extraordinarily lax with regard to proper behavior and yet were strangely proud of themselves, without exception. I say strange because all of the foreigners were involved in businesses of borderline legality, and the Japanese women, not only in this hotel but in hotels everywhere, were making money every night from customers waylaid in their bars.

The hotel owner never seemed to understand these people. It is likely that his actual comprehension of them was even more limited than he himself acknowledged. He was able to confide only in me. The life story he related while we were sitting beside the heater began in a mumbling voice but ended in tones of great pride. It ran roughly as follows.

When quite young, he left his parents' poor home in Kakogawa and went to Tokyo, dreaming the typical dream of worldly success. By the time he arrived in Tokyo, all he had left was a single fifty-sen coin. From that time onward he did any kind of work he could find, and eventually ended up a clerk in a whorehouse in Yoshiwara, where he discovered that the world of prostitution was just the avenue to easy 'success' he had been searching for.

How a clerk in his twenties could become the owner of a whorehouse in Yoshiwara within ten years is still a mystery to me. He was never willing to reveal the details of the affair. It goes without saying that it could only happen through unmentionable, underhanded means. He eventually became as wealthy as he had ever desired to be. But just about that time Japan rushed unreasonably into war, and when black clouds began to gather over the future of prostitution, he sold the whorehouse without a moment's delay and obtained the hotel in Kobe with part of the money from the sale.

Drunk on the story of his own success, he even took the trouble to show me photographs from his Yoshiwara days. These were all, without exception, photos of tarted-up whores with the pig himself posing in the midst of them in a lordly manner. Smiling with pleasure, he showed these photos to the women of the hotel as well. To his blank amazement, every time the women (who themselves earned money by sleeping with men) examined one of these pictures, they would exchange significant glances, their faces expressing an unvoiced, 'Hmmm.' They made no effort whatsoever to hide their contempt for the exploiter. Thoroughly unable to understand such a show of antipathy, his broad, ugly face, which had just been swollen with pride, seemed to shrink suddenly to the next smaller size. Lost in a cloud, he withdrew to his room.

Though he had no head for dealing with his boarders, there was nothing wrong with his ability to manage the assets of the hotel. Beginning with the first air raid in Tokyo, and practically every day thereafter, he removed items – from tableware in the storehouse to furniture in vacant guest rooms, even if they were only of slightly good quality – and carried them away to his parents' house in the countryside.

The women could not help but notice what he was doing. Convinced that the hotel was their home, their native sense of justice was outraged to the point where they felt compelled, as usual, to rush into my room to state their views. They declared that his having taken over the hotel with only a ten percent down payment did not give him the right to remove hotel property. They asked for something to be done about this. And all of them ended with the sigh, 'I feel sorry for Papa-san!'

Papa-san was our old white-haired manager, brother-in-law to the former owner, and as good-natured as a god. He had earned the nickname of John the Baptist from the way he would make the rounds in his free time with a hammer to make minor repairs to the rooms. This was indeed Kobe.

These high-spirited women had all had bad luck with fathers, so when they called him Papa-san, they did so from the bottom of their hearts.

I too was fond of the old man. But being unfamiliar with the law and ignorant of the actual details of the contract, I could not take up their cause. After that, I lost much of my reputation among the women. Actually, when my favorite rocking chair was carried away, I almost decided to fight against the pig myself, but I felt my courage crumble as I didn't want to upset the old manager.

The ex-whorehouse boss and now perplexed hotel owner was thus managing to gain the enmity of all the boarders. But then I witnessed something that, while enmity remained enmity, awakened a feeling in me that was very close to pity.

There were only two Japanese men among the boarders – the

superintendent of a sanitarium and myself. One day, a youth from Tokyo, who one might call fabulously handsome, appeared unexpectedly at the hotel and became a boarder. He did not seem to have anything resembling a job, and took instead to haunting the kitchen, where the owner's wife of around thirty years of age (she was more than he deserved, by the way) was always working with a happy smile.

I was usually the only one who ate in his own room. Most of the boarders at the hotel, regardless of the time, ate at a table in the corner of the kitchen. So it was impossible for the women of the hotel to miss the fact that the attractive youth always lingered near the comely wife. Consequently, the youth's reputation around the hotel suffered because he had eyes only for the wife and treated the other ten or so self-proclaimed beauties as though they were completely beneath his notice.

Such cosmopolitan women might have put up with anything, but could not help feeling piqued at being considered unworthy of even the slightest attention. To make matters worse, the barmaids of Kobe had a tendency to feel an irrational attraction to men from Tokyo. Before long, the atmosphere of the hotel seemed to burn with a weird and sultry flame.

The identity of the youth from Tokyo was soon brought to light by a visit from a plainclothes military police officer, who appeared about a month after the young man had taken up residence in the hotel.

At the time, I happened to be with him at the counter carrying on a discussion about Tokyo. The MP, mistaking the young man for a clerk, asked if a person named such-and-such from Tokyo was residing at the hotel. Saying, 'Let me ask the manager,' he walked away calmly, and though the policeman continued to wait, he never returned. Beginning to get suspicious after some time had passed, the MP asked me if the young man had been a clerk. When I told him that he was a boarder, the policeman shouted, 'Damn it!' and ran down the passage into which the young man had disappeared. But the building had many doors for the convenience of couples who wished to be discreet, and he had already made his getaway. It turned out he had fled Tokyo to avoid being drafted.

Within less than ten days the youth sauntered back into the hotel and, as before, continued to play up to the wife in the kitchen. To my great surprise, the MPs paid no further attention to him. In those days Kobe was simply crawling with spies, and our rubbish-heap hotel was being closely watched at all times. But though the MPs appeared almost every day, they must have had more important cases to pursue. The draft-dodger was ignored and left to dillydally in the kitchen.

For the owner of the hotel, who was experienced in the observation of such matters, it was impossible not to notice what was transpiring between his dear wife and the young man. Before long, he began to lug his hulking form into the kitchen, even though he normally disliked the place. Yet all he ever did there was observe the two quietly, his face cupped in his hands. It was as if he were being held hostage, not only by his love for the woman, but by his own guilt, of which she was only too aware. Consequently, she and her suitor remained unruffled and carried on their pleasant chats as usual.

After that, I regarded the former whorehouse boss in a different light.

Considered a nuisance by his wife, he was eventually driven out of the kitchen. Unable to join either the foreigners in the lobby or the Japanese women, who seemed nothing less than foreign themselves, he would sit out on the stone steps in front of the storehouse, playing with the ten or so hotel cats, just killing time.

The hotel owner's devotion to these cats was almost crazy. His characteristic parsimony vanished without a trace whenever he fed the cats the illicit meat purchased through the Egyptian boarder, Maged Elba. His huge body draped in a summer kimono embossed with the name of his former whorehouse, he would stroll along the corridors, leading a motley pack of flea-ridden cats like a festival crowd carrying a portable shrine. Though I had once felt disgust for this maniac and his cats, now that his wife had been stolen away from him – having become a cuckold – his agony, which he could confide to no one, was no longer funny but instead terribly pathetic. Perhaps I felt sympathy because I myself was at a complete loss over how to deal with Namiko, whom I had to watch carefully for fear she would go astray again.

I think there are few things as pitiful as a man whose beloved has been stolen. Unable to hate her, he continues to love her and is able to do nothing but curse himself. He wants to condemn the man who seduced her, but he knows that if the woman had not given freely of herself, such a situation would never have occurred. Any time his wife was not to be found, this giant cuckold took to prowling the hotel, looking to see where she might be, and he was always accompanied by his ten cats.

He did not even seem worried about the formations of B-29s, which were reducing one city after another to ashes, and sooner or later would do the same to Kobe.

Namiko, angered by the owner's insanity, ceased once and for all her flea-removing operations on the cats, which she had up to then been performing as though it were her job. She could not stand the owner's unwillingness to put his feelings aside. She was angry with me as well for my vague responses to her criticisms on the matter.

As for me, I am not sure when I first noticed the bewildering change in my attitude. I only know that I found myself feeling pity for a man I had once despised.

As we had expected, an air raid burned Osaka to the ground. Everyone knew that it was our turn next. In this tense atmosphere, I heard the wailing of the bulky hotel owner late one night as he stood in front of the door of the handsome youth's room. As the man wailed, so did the cats. My feet were heavy, but I could not abandon him now. As I approached, he could only point at the door and repeat, 'My wife, my wife.'

The next day, Namiko and I moved to a house on the hillside. Soon thereafter most of Kobe, including the hotel, was reduced to ashes. Only the storehouse was spared, but I heard that the heat and smoke killed about a dozen cats the hotel owner had locked up there before he fled. They were discovered in a heap pressed against the door.

I also heard that the owner returned to his parents' house in his hometown with both his wife and her lover, but that less than a month later he was pushed from a crowded train vestibule and killed.

§

The majority of the individuals who appear in this memoir, set in Kobe, passed away around the time of the war's conclusion. However, it is not accurate to say that I deliberately chose only those who died. It simply ended up that way on its own. As for why it turned out to be so, I myself don't know. The only thing I do know is that I hold deep affection for these deceased individuals in my heart.

[Serialized in *Haiku*, from the September 1954 issue to the June 1956 issue.]

KOBE SEQUEL

PREFACE

A few years ago, the general haiku magazine *Haiku* serialized ten pieces of my prose under the overall title of *Kobe*. They were my memoirs from the time I spent in Kobe from 1942 to 1946. All the people who appear in *Kobe* were good people, whether Japanese or not; at the same time, they were the people farthest away from 'a wartime state of emergency.' Like them, I believed that freedom was the highest reason for being alive, and I therefore had a deep interest in their ways of living. To my surprise, *Kobe* attracted many admirers. Someone even presented me with a plan to make it into a movie.

Now, the editor-in-chief of *Tenrō* (Dog Star) keeps pushing me for sequels to *Kobe*. However, there have been huge changes between the time when I wrote the ten episodes of *Kobe* and the present as regards both where and how I live. In addition, being old and lazy, the fountain of my pen has dried up. I doubt that the second part of my prodigal memoirs will gain even a bit of the reader's attention; but, in hope of getting him or her to smile even once in 'this painful world,' I'm going to narrate foolish stories, full of shameful episodes. As in my previous book, I have completely excluded all fiction from the content. Therefore, I beg the reader never, ever to suspect me of fabrication, as Seishi Sensei once did.

One day in May 1959, Tokyo's evening newspaper carried a detailed article about a woman whose life had served as the basis for a novel by Niwa Fumio. It was filmed by the Daiei Movie Company under the title *Fighting Fish at Night*, starring Kyō Machiko. I had neither read the book nor seen the film, and yet I became absorbed in the article because in the accompanying photograph I recognized a woman I had once known very well.

ABOUT A LADY

According to the article she was thirty-nine years old and the proprietor of 'C,' a nightclub in Akasaka that is reputed to draw revenues of one million yen a night. She had a husband who was part Chinese, and was the mother of one child.

Among nightclubs in Tokyo, there are two or three considered first class. The patrons are almost all foreigners, including those from Japan's former Asian possessions. The money they spend is paid out of the expense accounts and campaign funds of Japanese businessmen with political affiliations; thus, the more they dawdle over a reparations problem or the selection of new airplanes for national defense, the richer the nightclubs become.

The article estimated that 'One night's revenue amounts to one million yen,' but I know this figure must be much lower than is actually the case. I once accompanied Tōgō Seiji, a painter, his wife and their daughter Tamami, Yokoyama Hakkō, a haiku poet, and Abe Kongō, also a painter, to another nightclub. We didn't get away for less than ten thousand yen per person. I cannot believe that a nightclub like that has only one hundred customers per evening, so the real revenue must be three times as much as the reported million, and over a month it would be as high as one hundred million.

How much money a nightclub makes is none of my concern, but if the lady in charge turns out to be someone I know, that's a different story.

It was in December 1942 that I became a boarder in the dilapidated hotel on Tor Road in Kobe. Without repeating myself too much, I shall briefly sum up the sequence of events: I had escaped from Tokyo and my family, and was in search of a place to live. With that in mind, I went to a bar and asked a woman there for suggestions. She ended up giving me a letter of introduction to C—ko of the international hotel – C—ko, the million-yen-a-night madam of today.

The following day I called on C—ko. Raucous jazz could be heard through the door, even though Japan had declared war upon the United States and Britain the year before and playing American music was considered unpatriotic. This seemed to sum up the very essence of what makes Kobe, Kobe – or so I thought as I waited there. Finally, the door opened and C—ko looked out at me skeptically. I discovered later that I was the only person who had ever called on her with a letter of introduction, and by this simple act of courtesy, I had earned her long-lasting favor.

As soon as she understood my reason for being there, she introduced me to the reception clerk, selected a room key, and guided me on a tour of the hotel. From that day and for more than a year afterward, I was a resident of that peculiar hotel-cum-boardinghouse, where the only two Japanese men in residence were myself and the director of a sanitarium. The seven Japanese women at the hotel all worked in bars, including C—ko, who was only twenty-five but already running a bar in Kano-cho. Besides the Japanese, there was an Egyptian (who was always under surveillance, being a citizen of an enemy nation), a White Russian, and a Turkish-Tartar, among other foreigners. The lobby was always full of people who were somehow managing to eat, even during wartime, though how I could not begin to imagine. The nature of their varied businesses was clear only for the women working in bars, 'clear' because it was common knowledge, even from prewar days, that the women in Kobe's bars were in the business of spending the night with customers.

As I have confessed before, no sooner had I settled into this hotel than I fell into a relationship with Namiko from Yokohama. Since we were the only Japanese couple living together in this place, it was not long before our two rooms were transformed into a private club, from sometime past noon, when the late-rising ladies got up, until evening.

Out of this group, C—ko was the most conspicuous. In the cosmopolitan atmosphere of Kobe, becoming the proprietress of a bar at the age of twenty-five required considerable pluck and intelligence, and above all else, great physical beauty.

Sometimes we would dance in the lobby. Although C—ko's face would be level with mine, her body was short and her legs were long, which made her center of gravity high. Consequently, she was difficult to dance with. When dancing with her women friends, C—ko would always take the lead, and expected to do the same when dancing with me. She would stride about with long-legged steps, all the while pressing against me with her huge bosom.

For whatever reason, Kobe's bar girls had an unfathomable weakness for Tokyo men. C—ko had a handsome young lover from Tokyo who visited her in Kobe. He had seduced her by pretending to be a novelist. He would sit beside the heater in the lobby saying things like, 'The royalties haven't arrived from Tokyo yet,' knowing very well that the words impressed C—ko and made the other women feel awe and respect for him. He had been told that I was nothing but a businessman, so he was at ease bragging. But I knew that he had not written a single manuscript, and would never receive a single cent in royalty payments. He was just a man who had left his wife and children in the suburbs of Tokyo to lead a dissolute life in the freedom of Kobe. If he had actually been a novelist, observing and noting the extraordinary lifestyles of the people in that hotel during the war, he would not have been so single-minded in his pursuit of carnal pleasures. However, this handsome youth did occasionally return to Tokyo to make money.

C—ko usually returned home at about two o'clock in the morning, blind drunk, and pummelled on the door to my room. She would beg Namiko for a midnight snack and give me her large handbag full of banknotes for safekeeping until the next day.

Her own room had a double bed, and who knows with what sort of midnight callers she might be sharing it. Even if she opened her bed to strangers, the contents of her handbag had to be secured.

Whenever her lover was back in Tokyo, C—ko was obliged to give her favors to the plainclothes military police, the police inspectors of the foreign affairs section, and other officials. These men would drink at her bar until they were positively ill, and then return to her bed at the hotel. Such perks were free, of course.

For C—ko, these things were daily matters, and for some ten years they had been her only form of taxation. Though they treated her badly, the fact was that she was the one keeping them as pets and not the other way around.

C—ko was born in a seaside village in Yamaguchi prefecture, but having lost her parents in her early years, she was raised by her grandmother. Ever since she was a child, she had possessed an Amazon spirit and enjoyed above all else teasing the boys and making them cry. She spent the summer in the sea from morning to night, but at the age of fourteen, as she lay on a rock by the shore, tired from swimming, a quiet flow of blood had appeared from between her thighs. The boys were astonished and accompanied her back to her home. There, her grandmother prepared festive red-bean rice and lit a candle before the tablet of the dead on the household altar. Riveted by the sense of mystery, the boys had crowded into the doorway, watching C—ko and the old woman.

The spring she turned sixteen, a well-built C—ko came to Kobe and began working in a bar. That very first day, a sailor from a foreign ship had 'made her a woman.' In the fewer than ten years since then, she had come to be known as 'Kobe's C—ko.' She had nothing to fear but her granny in the village on the Inland Sea.

When C—ko came home intoxicated, she would often fall asleep in the living room of my apartment. Later, dripping water from her shower, she would get me to dry her off with a big bath towel. 'Namiko, excuse me!' she would giggle, and Namiko would laugh, too. After C—ko fell asleep – it was often as late as three o'clock in the morning – I would sometimes be awakened by her talking in her sleep in the next room. Most of the time it was a wild sort of English, but occasionally she would say 'O-bā-chan,' the Japanese word for 'Granny.'

She was well-proportioned, and had a look of dignity despite her youth. She was also very ambitious. 'In time, I will get my big chance,' she often told me. Words such as 'self-reliance' and 'independence' fell from her lips, quite unlike what usually escaped the mouths of Kobe's women. It was not just talk either. She always seized an opportunity.

Although normally shrewd, C—ko's weakness was her fondness for men; she couldn't help herself. Before the Tokyo writer, there was Sakurai Kiyoshi of the Sakurai Orchestra. Whenever Sakurai appeared on stage in Osaka, she let him stay overnight. Food by that time was scarce in the city, so where did she obtain the ingredients for the thick egg omelettes she made for her violinist? I never did find out. C—ko would use my kitchen, where she prepared soup stock from dried bonito to dilute the eggs which she then cooked in a frying pan little by little and layered into stacks. She worked with her left hand, her only utensil a table knife.

Jam-packed into the box lunch of the Sakurai conductor were many delicacies unobtainable in either Tokyo or Osaka. She would cheerfully deliver it herself, traveling between Kobe and Osaka.

Once, when her Tokyo 'novelist' lover had stayed away far too long to suit her, she began saying, 'I will get him down here even if I have to put a rope around his neck and drag him.' She wanted me to go with her, 'in case he says no.' I was very reluctant to return to Tokyo, which I had escaped with no small effort, and only by traveling in the most decrepit, boarded-up train. Still, Namiko wanted to see her mother in Yokohama, so the three of us ended up riding together as far as Yokohama.

I summoned the young 'novelist' to the Grand Hotel and, in

C—ko's company, told him of her feelings. He promised to return. The next day C—ko, Namiko and I clattered back to Kobe. That one night with her lover seemed to satisfy her; soon after arriving in Kobe, she went wild over the son of some rich family in Osaka.

At times like this she always pulled me into the maelstrom, using me to solve the inevitable complications of her love affairs. My stupidly sympathetic feelings were completely transparent. So when the youth from Tokyo put in his dashing appearance, the wealthy scion was already in C—ko's locked room. She dashed into my room and hid in the bed, as the two rivals swarmed into my apartment. All three were utterly speechless. I was also struck dumb. Only Namiko continued to calmly pick fleas off a cat.

The next day, C—ko got what she deserved. The 'novelist' shaved her delta with his razor and returned to Tokyo. C—ko went to the trouble of showing Namiko what had happened. It seems she had borrowed a calligraphy brush and inkstone to temporarily camouflage the problem.

When the war ended I was living in a cavernous, Western-style mansion on the hillside, the only area that had escaped the fires. C—ko, as well as the other women from the hotel, arrived as refugees, so I fed them by prematurely digging up the potatoes I had grown at the expense of a flower bed. When those were about gone, good-natured men began appearing out of nowhere, each of them bearing food for the women. A month later, like the receding tide, the women disappeared one by one.

The house had two rooms upstairs, three downstairs, plus a servant's room the size of eight tatami mats. The rooms were big, more than ten tatami, and the main hall exceptionally so, more than twenty tatami. They commanded a sweeping view of the burnt-out expanse of Kobe. Just as I was thinking that it was rather wasteful to share all of this only with Namiko, C—ko as usual recognized a good opportunity.

One day she appeared at the house in the company of a friend (who was the temporary wife of an Italian), silently held out a bundle of banknotes, and grinned at me. According to her plan, if she were to sublet this huge, European-style house from me, the spacious rooms divided up into small ones would make a nice hotel. Since the American Army had already been stationed in Kobe, she thought that by providing them with a hotel and liquor, she could earn great amounts of money; and, since 'Sensei' was conveniently able to speak English, I would be perfect to serve as a manager for the present. 'But,' she stated calmly, 'Leave all the rest to us women.'

The war was over, but my own prospects were none too bright, and ten thousand yen was a blessing. Being a hotel manager wouldn't be so bad; I had already tried being a dentist and a businessman. I agreed, and the ten thousand yen was used up in no time.

C—ko and her friend brought in carpenters and other workmen, and the plans for the Hillside Hotel were well under way by the time I learned that the employees of the hotel would all be women and that they would be living there too. I was shocked. C—ko was planning to open a brothel and I was on the road to becoming the manager of a house of ill-repute. Never mind about everyone (including me) starting over again.... I asked C—ko for an annulment of the contract.

'That's why Sensei is a failure,' she said, looking at Namiko. Namiko appeared to be of the same opinion. Moreover, having canceled the contract, the ten thousand yen that I'd received but had already spent was forfeited as well. Given a one month margin, I was barely able to return it, though the way I made the money is something I can no longer remember.

In the autobiographical novel Sawaki Kin'ichi wrote, there is a person from Kobe who resembles me, posing as the manager of a cabaret. This seems to be a story written prematurely about the Hillside Hotel, which vanished before it came into being. My cowardice prevented me from turning a dangerous corner, which is why I have been exposed to only gentle hazards since.

With the failure of her brothel, C—ko gave up such pursuits and gave birth to the child of a German sailor. It was her first, but before long the father returned to his native land, and the baby was passed along to her granny. Soon after marrying her husband, C—ko was again running bars in both Tokyo and Kobe, finally carrying out her original intention by becoming the manager of a first-rate nightclub in Tokyo.

I have not seen her since the Hillside Hotel days, but after all that's happened, can she truly say, 'I have succeeded?' Probably not.

THREE MAIDENS

During the war the city of Kobe was a veritable wellspring of rumors and false reports, that is to say, it was a haven for spies. Consequently, the foreign affairs section of the prefectural office was always in a frantic state, as people of enemy and allied nations alike spread word of Japan's imminent defeat. No matter how government radio broadcasts trumpeted the victory of each battle, by the way German and Italian sailors lounged around in Kobe, the people of the city all knew their submarines were blockaded by the enemy.

The surprising fact was that, time and again, information based on hearsay proved in the end not only to be mostly true, but in fact conservative. As a matter of fact, one of my relatives, a doctor running a mental hospital to whom I used to go to receive rice and sugar, told me without even bothering to lower his voice that in the straits of Kitan, American submarines were on alert on round-the-clock shifts. This was in 1944, and I later heard the same report from an officer of a German submarine.

By then, I was already scraping the bottom of the barrel to find and deliver supplies to my customers; I had grown accustomed to traveling between Tokyo and Kobe on trains filled to bursting with travelers. Once it was so congested that I had the experience of spending several hours on the steps at the end of the car while hanging onto the outside of the train.

One day in the summer of 1944, Wada Hensuirō came to my house on Yamamoto Street, bringing a beautiful girl for whom he asked me to assume responsibility. As I listened, he explained that she was working for the Osaka railway bureau to escape being drafted as a laborer in Himeji, where her father was a deputy stationmaster.

'Commuting every day on those murderous trains is such a pain, and your house is full of empty rooms ... it's just right. You could keep her and take good care of her,' he said.

The prospect of having a girl who resembled the film star Takamine Hideko become a member of my desolate family was something that I certainly would not oppose. But Namiko had developed a strong dislike of other women after her life of prostitution in Yokohama, and I was afraid she would not agree to this arrangement under any circumstances. The girl was very wise, however, and during the conversation between Hensuirō and me, she very easily made a favorable impression on Namiko.

Until Kiyoko came to live with us, the life Namiko and I led was a bleak and cheerless one. I was living without purpose; Namiko had a mother and younger brothers to support in Yokohama. Because she had worked to support herself since she was a girl, it was very difficult for her to deal with the reality of life with me in Kobe. 'Don't be swayed by emotions,' was her secret daily invocation; however, its effectiveness weakened day by day, to a point which vexed her, and turned her against me. It was a long, long, black, black night.

Kiyoko changed our life drastically. In the dark, European-style mansion, the lunar nature of Namiko and the sunny disposition of Kiyoko created new balance and harmony. Perhaps Namiko thought an attachment between the beautiful Kiyoko and me could provide an escape for her. No matter how much Namiko might have desired this, it was impossible, for Kiyoko was betrothed to a student at Kobe Commercial College who had volunteered as a pilot in Kasumigaura and Kariya and was now a second lieutenant.

Kiyoko was light-hearted, fond of flashiness, and at first glance looked like a flapper, but in her affection for this second lieutenant there was unusual depth. As part of a kamikaze unit, his life could literally be called one without a tomorrow. Although the betrothed couple were kept far apart, it was certainly natural under the circumstances that their emotions should burn so steadily.

Every Saturday, Kiyoko would travel to wherever her fiancé was stationed: Kasumigaura, Kariya, Kanoya, one after the other. Alone, she journeyed all the way to Ibaraki, Aichi, and Kagoshima prefectures. I don't know how these two young people spent their time together, but Kiyoko would always return to Kobe as thin as a rail. Perhaps it was partly the exhaustion of train travel.

Namiko, like a floating water plant in both heart and body, showed a gentle sympathy to Kiyoko; to Namiko who had lost all passion, Kiyoko's whole-hearted love affair must have seemed quite an enviable and priceless thing.

Promoted to first lieutenant in Kanoya, Kyushu, the young man was dispatched to Okinawa, never to return. The lieutenant's parents and siblings were living in Kobe. So, after they received official notice of the dispatch, Kiyoko visited their home every day, hoping for a further communication from the government.

'There's a one in ten thousand chance he's been washed up on the shore of some isolated island.... I often have such dreams,' she told me, and though her face held a smile, her eyes shed abundant tears.

After the defeat, Kiyoko wanted to know, at whatever cost, the details surrounding her fiancé's death. She went alone to Tokyo to check at the Ministry of the Navy, but in preparation for the enemy landing on the mainland all documents had been placed in a tunnel-like warehouse carved into the mountains of Shinshū.

Standing in a train all the way from Tokyo to Shinshū, Kiyoko demonstrated pure will power. Hungry and exhausted, she finally arrived in the depths of the mountain … and fainted on the spot.

To locate one person's records in the massive files took her and the man in charge an entire day. According to the document, on a certain day and month in the sea near Okinawa, in command of a squadron of kamikaze planes, the pilot's fate had been sealed.

Kiyoko recovered herself after sleeping for a day on her return to Kobe.

Two years later she married a young doctor. The day before the ceremony she called at my house and stayed the night. She said it was because my house was closer than Himeji to the location of the wedding ceremony in Osaka. The real reason, I suspect, was that she wanted to bid a final farewell to the dead pilot's spirit, which she had brought back with her each time she went to see him.

Our Western-style house was built back in the early Meiji era and was undoubtedly crowded with the ghosts of foreigners, so I am sure that the ghost of the Japanese pilot was feeling right at home.

After the war, American troops began to move in from the Philippines. Around the Kinki area, the first landing was in Wakayama prefecture. It seemed only a matter of time before they would appear in Kobe. Rumors spread concerning the imagined behavior of the conquerors toward the conquered, especially toward the women. There were some parents who even sent their daughters to the nearby countryside.

One day a young woman from a neighboring civil defense unit called on me, since I had once been an air-raid squad captain.

'My husband is a chief engineer on a ship and is not home, but I know about those beastly Americans from Western films, and won't they come barging in and …' – the lady used the word 'rape' clearly.

Although I was embarrassed to answer, I replied that in a city such as Kobe these things would hardly ever happen, but the voluptuous lady was not satisfied with that and persisted with further questions, including, 'Can the captain guarantee the safety …' How could I give such a promise? Fortunately, the nearby Fuji Hotel became a billet for the military government team, so the peace and public order of the neighborhood was maintained.

I myself had stayed in the Fuji Hotel before the war – I think it was around 1938. At the time, I was in love with a young woman in Tokyo, a chaste relationship of some five years' standing. She had contracted a slight chest ailment and had been sent to Beppu in Kyushu for her health; after she began to feel better she decided to return home. I came from Tokyo then to meet her on the wharf in Kobe.

Meeting in Kobe instead of Tokyo after this three-month lapse, we decided to stay in the quiet Fuji Hotel. Air-raid drills had already begun all over the nation, so the view of the city from the hotel balcony was a sea of darkness. The autumn night was filled with the competing chirps of insects, and moonlight dripped from the night sky like water.

Suddenly, a lion roared in nearby Suwayama Zoo. At that, we retired to separate rooms and spent a virtuous night. These are that night's haiku:

> Air-raid drill –
> I caress
> her moonlit fingers

> In Kobe
> a lion's roar – we sleep
> in separate hotel rooms

About two hundred soldiers were billeted at the Fuji Hotel. One day about a week after they were stationed there, two soldiers spotted me standing by the gate to my house and made gestures of opening and drinking from a bottle, shouting, 'Beer! Beer!'

Before moving into this house I had stayed for a long time in the hotel on Tor Road and knew that German and Italian soldiers were always wanting beer, so thinking that these American soldiers, too, wanted to buy some drinks, I signaled them to enter the house, where I had been keeping bottles of beer in case I needed to trade them for food.

These men turned out to be sellers, not buyers. In their jackets were many large pockets from which bottles of beer appeared as if by magic, one after the other, and now stood crowded together on the table. All of it was Japanese. I suppose the city of Kobe had presented them to the military government.

When we realized that both sides were sellers, we all burst out laughing. From that night on, these two, plus one more fellow, came almost every night to my home for amusement.

Luther was an optimistic giant from Oklahoma, a high school graduate who had worked in the oil fields. Marques was a Mexican-American, lewd, with a dark complexion and a dark nature to match. He had only finished junior high and had been a tractor driver on a farm in California. Milhorn was the youngest of the three, a German-American who wore square, rimless glasses. He was a college student whose hometown I never learned.

These three kept one another's company because they were all on KP duty, which meant they were cooks, peelers of potatoes, cutters of onions, and so on, and were generally treated with disdain by the others. I learned later that when a soldier is punished, he is demoted to KP, an abbreviation for Kitchen Police but in fact a euphemism for being a cook on duty.

They had experienced battles in the Philippines, and knew that the Japanese military authorities had been the real enemy and the victims had been the common people. They seemed to have a pretty clear understanding of the general situation.

My odd household could hardly be called a real home, but it was an easy-going sort of place where the men could come and go with their shoes on and make themselves understood in their own language. The advantage to me was that by knowing these three, who had come from such different backgrounds before becoming soldiers, I could get a better picture of the American way of thinking.

There is an adage that says one should not drink from a stolen fountain, but it is my principle to drink without apology when I'm thirsty from whatever source is available, stolen or otherwise. So I ate American food without hesitation and quaffed my share of tasteless American beer.

In time young Milhorn was assigned to mail duty and it became his job to go to headquarters every day in a jeep to pick up the mail. That the college student was made a mailman might be taken as a comment on his efficiency as a soldier.

One day this mailman picked up a sailor down at the port and delivered him to my home. The sailor wanted to send a letter to a girl he had become acquainted with in Wayakama, and he wanted me to write it for him. One can always ask Uncle Saitō for such favors – knowing this, the intellectual soldier with the rimless glasses took the trouble to bring the fellow to my house by jeep. It was the same old story.

The young woman had been minding a tobacco shop on a corner in Wakayama. The twenty-year-old sailor had appeared at the shop every day and eventually made friends with her, but his language skills didn't pass muster.

What he wanted to say in his letter was basically that his ship was anchored in the harbor at Kobe, and that he wanted her to come see him, guided by a certain Japanese whose name was written on the envelope. This Japanese was to be me.

The trains running between Wakayama and Osaka were so crowded that once a grown man's ribs had been crushed and broken. There was no guarantee for the safety of ribs on the trains between Osaka and Kobe either, but it was on just such a train that the young woman came one day to call at my house.

She was nineteen, small in stature, and with a face as round as a tray. She could not be considered beautiful. Taking her to the wharf, we began to visit the row of battleships, one after another, as they lay at anchor, and at last located the young sailor, George, who told us he could come ashore the following day.

Like a child he entreated me to translate for him: 'Thank you for coming from such a distance. I wanted to see you with all my heart, and since I am coming ashore as soon as I possibly can, please wait for me. I love you from the bottom of my heart.'

The young woman dropped her head in embarrassment

while listening to such words spoken by an 'old uncle' she had met for the first time that day. But when I finished, she looked up smiling into the sailor's face. I did not think it odd, but at the same time I felt an absolute sense of sorrow. The one who was absurd in this scene was me.

From that day on, the young woman became my house guest When the sailor came to meet her, they would shut themselves up in a room, so silent that not a sound could be heard. Since they had no common language, this silence was perfectly natural.

One day the young woman confided, looking both thoughtful and desperate, that she could not continue to stay at my house forever and that she was getting a futon from Wakayama and renting a room nearby. To my surprise, she said that her elder brother was bringing the futon from Wakayama the same day. To come carrying a futon on one of those jam-packed trains, and to change trains at Osaka as well, seemed all but impossible to me, but this was only the concern of a frail, fifty-year-old man. Her elder brother, perspiring liberally even though it was winter, came up Yamamoto Street from Sannomiya Station with her luggage on his back. When I spoke with him, he told me that the family was going to let her do as she wished.

Up until then I had kept my opinions to myself, but in the earnest attitude of the two young people there was no trace of flippancy whatsoever, and I began to worry all the more about the time when the ship would have to depart. At this point, I called the girl into a separate room and asked her just how intimate the relationship was.

She replied, 'No more than kissing. He asked for sex, but I'm too afraid to allow it.'

I believed her. So, speaking as her old uncle, I gave her some standard advice, such as, 'If you rent a room just for two, you will no longer be a virgin, and you will also never know when the ship will depart, probably never to return … What will happen if you become pregnant?' and so on.

The girl listened to me with her head bowed, without tears.

When I fell silent, she answered, 'I understand very well, and though it is hard, I will put a stop to this.'

Next it was the sailor's turn. I told him in straightforward language to get a reverend from the ship and hold a marriage ceremony, today and now, and Uncle Saitō would stand as witness. At this he sadly hung his head with his chin sunk onto his breast.

Again the two closeted themselves in a room, as quietly as small birds. They must have been bidding one another a wordless farewell.

The next day the elder brother, whom she had summoned by telegram, took her home on that hideous train, her futon again on his back. The north wind blew that day in a raging gale.

A few days later, with snow fluttering down like powder, the sailor came to bid me farewell before his ship left. He thanked me for the consideration I had shown him, and quietly confided that he was glad he had not taken a room with the girl. I went to the gate to see him off, a child-like sailor in a coat reaching only to his waist, cheeks moistened with snow, teeth chattering in the cold.

'Take it easy!' I shouted to him as he walked away. 'I will,' he answered, turning to look back.

HAIKU ONCE AGAIN

The food provisions in Kobe during the war could not have been much different from what was distributed in other cities, but since it was a haven for black marketeers, unusual goods often turned up.

When Mitani Akira, who had been sent into the Kure Marine Corps, popped in at my place, he was amazed to be served corned beef from Argentina. I retraced the route by which it had come into my hands: Maged Elba had sold it to me after exchanging it for two bottles of beer. A German submarine sailor named Otto had traded a shore leave for the corned beef. This corned beef had been acquired from a supply cruiser when a German submarine surfaced near Taiwan. This cruiser, when it had been near the coast of Africa, had fired on an Allied cargo ship coming by way of Cape Town, boarded the vessel, and looted the hold before it sank. According to Otto, submarines would sometimes put to sea and commit acts of piracy such as this. Especially clever sailors were appointed to robbery duty, with specialists for certain items: whisky, canned goods, raw meat, flour, sugar, etc. If these were successfully obtained, each specialist received a one-percent bonus. Thus, by using only one of his three allotted shore leaves, Otto managed to obtain corned beef from a buddy who had been on canned goods robbery detail.

Articles arriving by such strange routes circulated almost openly in Kobe but, as everywhere in Japan, the only officially distributed rations just before the end of the war were rice bran and wheat bran. At distribution time, my Chinese friend Won would appear with a large sack to collect the bran. He would then bow a hundred times and say thank-you over and over as he left. Two or three days later he would return with perhaps three small chicken eggs, saying, 'These are Sensei's eggs.'

Though he appeared foolish, he was highly businesslike, and kept about ten chickens. While rice and wheat bran continued to be distributed, he was actually making a profit by trading in chicken feed.

There had been a rumor circulating in Kobe since around the first of August that surrender had finally been decided (a shortwave receiver must have been hidden somewhere), but matters became clear to me only on the fifteenth of August as I listened to the strange intonations of the Emperor's broadcast.

Two or three days later, while I was standing vacantly in my garden, two yellow training planes from the Japanese Army appeared with a stuttering roar from the east, and vanished as quickly into the west. It was only then, touched by the valor of those pathetic planes, that I finally shed a few tears.

Why were these two training planes still flying in the days following the surrender? Were they young officers sworn to fight a decisive battle to the finish in the interior of Japan? Or were they just escaping with a souvenir stolen from some military depot? Whatever the reason, tears rolled slowly down my cheeks.

At about this time, as he often did in those days, Wada Hensuirō visited me from Nagoya. His big, close-cropped head was bowed. Since Hensuirō was not one who would feel desperate or disappointed about defeat in war, I asked him what was troubling him. He told me that the Potsdam Conference had decided that all leaders would face trial as war criminals, including newspapermen of more than middle standing.

'I, too, am of more than middle standing,' he said.

We were already wearied by our experience of being arrested and confined to a small room in 1940, so I was greatly worried for his sake. In any event, nothing happened to him after all. He never had the chance to go before the American Military Tribunal and use the English he had learned in his English literature class at Kyoto University.

Around the twentieth of August, some ship-based American planes appeared in the skies over Kobe and dropped materials attached to parachutes over the prefectural office. There were some who remarked smugly that the Americans were dropping food to yesterday's enemy, but I heard that in fact the materials were clearly addressed to a certain prisoner-of-war camp, with notices attached stating that anyone caught looting would be shot.

On that very day, a group of village leaders from the surrounding districts was hurrying to the prefectural office for a meeting following the defeat. One of them was killed outright by a direct hit from one of these air drops. With the war and the air raids over, this particular casualty was, as far as I know, the unluckiest victim of the war.

Harai-san continued to live at my house on Yamamoto Street, a desperately lonely person who had been driven out of her hotel by an air raid. The description of Harai-san as a desperately lonely person is my own. She herself seemed to be of the opinion that being a woman was as good as having a million yen, regardless of whether she was burned out of house and home by an air raid, or if a war was lost. As long as men did not become extinct, she was convinced that sun and food would pursue her, so she remained unconcerned.

Five days after the manna for the war prisoners dropped from the sky, Harai-san returned home at midnight. Saying, 'It's a souvenir,' she gave me a grass-colored shirt and trousers – an army outfit. Since the black-market street stalls had not yet appeared, I questioned the source. Simpering as usual, she said she had been given them at a party. To my surprise, she had attended a celebration for American prisoners of war, held only ten days after the defeat. The shirt and trousers provided for the prisoners had originally been made for Japanese soldiers; in a corner of the room where the party was held, the old uniforms, shirts, and other articles had been removed and discarded, creating a mountainous pile.

'So on the way out, I picked them up without saying anything and came home,' she said in a relaxed manner.

Harai-san was drunk on American rum and went to bed in high spirits, humming the same tune she always did when she got drunk: 'That's why I warned you, didn't I?' For her, new men had appeared – as many as she could sweep out and throw away.

Japan's rationed goods were so bad that the Occupation Army began to distribute food brought from the Philippines and rations from the front lines. They also distributed butter and cheese. I guess they were trying to tame the bizarre Japanese with food. Of the American rations, the one that lasted the longest was corn, first rationed as uncooked grain. My next-door neighbor, a White Russian named Mr. Vasikov, was always exasperated by this corn, which was as hard as pebbles, and always threw it, still in the bag, into the street. Just then Mr. Won would appear, as though he had been waiting; as he retrieved the bag, he would bow his head a hundred times toward Vasikov's house, saying *aigato, aigato* – his way of pronouncing *arigatō* (thank you) – before turning to go.

We wondered how the American Army, which had no horses, could possibly have had enough horse feed to distribute all over Japan; no, in fact this corn was something Japan had actually paid to import from the winning side. I did not learn this until later. At the time, everyone assumed that the Americans were giving it away for nothing. Since corn as hard as stone cannot be eaten either boiled or fried, they began distributing it as cornmeal, but no one knew how to prepare the yellow powder either.

It just so happened that Namiko's colleague from Yokohama days, Yuri, was living in a house in the hills of Kobe. She was the Japanese wife of an ex-captain of a German passenger line. This captain was a fine gentleman of about fifty. He did not associate with other Germans living in Kobe, nor go to clubs. Namiko and I were his only friends.

Before the war this captain had run a sight-seeing boat for a first-class steamship company in Hamburg, his routes including the fjords of Norway, and the coasts of Africa and Italy.

Since the beginning of the war in Europe he had been in Mexico. From there he had crossed the waters to Japan, where he was employed as the captain of an Imperial ship on the Taiwan sea route, but at the time we were acquainted he had no ship, so while on land he doted on his young Japanese wife.

I imagine he was probably Jewish, and that's why he had escaped Germany to seek a peaceful life in Mexico. It was a Japanese embassy official who brought him to Japan. In those days there was already a shortage of captains for requisitioned ships, so I suppose the embassy official persuaded him to accept an invitation. Being Jewish, it seems natural that he chose not to associate with the Germans in Kobe.

This old sea captain knew how to process the good-for-nothing cornmeal into delicious bread. In order to demonstrate his method and teach it to Namiko, he appeared in my kitchen, where in no time at all he managed to bake golden cornbread. He told me he had learned the method in Mexico.

Though I knew he was a wanderer, I was still greatly surprised and filled with admiration to know that a captain serving the largest steamship company in Germany had made the effort to learn the recipe for cornbread, which is a daily staple in Mexico.

He also taught me to make five different potato dishes, one of which made it possible to do without rice, a priceless commodity in those days. Two potatoes, one spoonful of wheat flour, and a bit of oil made enough pancakes for one person; these German-style pancakes often appear on the dining table of my poor home to this day.

Whether it was before or after the war that the couple was able to collect on their fire insurance, I cannot remember; I've even forgotten whether the amount of payment was ten or twenty percent, but I do recall that the captain and Yuri, under separate names, had each put five thousand yen into a household insurance policy. From the time they made their claim until payment was received at the Kobe branch of the Nippon Bank, the captain was always with me.

The line at the assessment office had been interminable. After half a day the captain's turn finally came, but when the couple admitted to the officials that they were husband and wife though they used different names, they were told they could only receive insurance payment for one person. Repeated arguments seemed to have no effect. We spent many hours there day after day until we finally received an insurance settlement for two. This was achieved thanks to a certificate of appreciation which had been given to the captain during his Taiwan sea route days by the Ladies' Patriotic Society of Taipei.

The captain seemed grateful to be receiving even a part of his insurance money, and he tried to force me to accept ten percent of the settlement as a token of his gratitude, asking me to think of it as business. I stubbornly refused. Finally he brought me his white trousers, and asked me to at least take them as a small token. I accepted with gratitude. They were the only spare trousers he owned after being bombed out of his house. I gave these long and wide-legged trousers to Hensuirō, my tall friend, who was later able to wear them.

With the end of the war I once again began writing haiku, which I had not done since the summer of 1940. Since the repression of the New Rising Haiku movement, I had tried to find a new direction for my life. That blank period of five years was a time of introspection for the movement also, though I would never suggest this as a justification for repression. For me, this period allowed me to discover the connection between classical haiku, which I read in books kept on a shelf in an air-raid shelter, and the spirit of New Rising Haiku.

Since word spread to the haiku poets in the neighboring area that I was living in Kobe, several poets began calling on me each day. Suzuki Murio, Izawa Tadao, and the Kobe members of the haiku magazine *Kanrai*, such as Hashizume Sajin and Hayashi Kaoru, all began holding regular monthly meetings at my house. Oka Isamu (from Tomioka-chō), Yasui Satsuki (from the eastern suburbs of Osaka), and Kurata Mizuyo (from Kōriyama), came without giving any thought to the inconvenience of having to change trains several times. The longest journey was taken by Kurata, who came from Kōriyama in Nara prefecture; during those days it was four hours one way, with three train changes.

Since Namiko had gone back to Yokohama, I was living

alone in the huge house. One cold day as sleet was falling, the impassioned young haiku poets gathered there as a group. I had neither charcoal nor firewood, so I struck down the board fence beside the garden and burnt it in my room for their sake. The damp wood smoldered, and all who came were hungry and wrapped in tatters. Our only comfort was the hot water we were drinking, yet our hearts glowed with good cheer. We were together, with no concern for the difference between haiku cliques, and knowing that we could once again write haiku made everyone feel at ease.

After the meeting Yasui, Kurata, and the others washed the cups in the kitchen. Already middle-aged, Yasui Satsuki's only desire was to become a member of the staff of *Kanrai*. Later this wish came true; not long after that, he died.

Suzuki Murio and Izawa Tadao were strong poets even then. Their tastes were quite different from those of the other haiku poets in Kobe; they founded *Seiten* with Nakamura Tamio, Shimazu Ryō, and Tateishi Toshio. I was surprised and pleased to find this group of lost New Rising Haiku poets in Osaka, and when they begged me to join them, I agreed.

It was also around this time that Hirahata Seitō, repatriated from a concentration camp in Shanghai, visited me from Kyoto, where he was posted. Wearing officer's trousers, and with the same stooped posture then as he has now, he walked down Yamamoto Street, examining the nameplate on each house. At the end of his long arm he held the postcard I had sent on which I'd drawn a map. From the time he first came into view more than a block away, I stood in front of my house and waited while he checked the houses one by one without ever looking my way. I waited without calling to him; watching him at the end of this five-year lapse, my heart flooded with feeling.

Seitō, whom I had not seen since the repression of the New Rising Haiku movement, had an even more dismal look than before, having undergone a series of hardships in the course of the war and as a prisoner of war.

In addition to the death of both his parents during the war, and concern for his wife and children, Seitō had much difficulty in his new start after repatriation to his homeland. He told me he would have to give up writing haiku.

For several hours, I delivered a fiery speech and urged him to change his mind. That such an excellent haiku poet as he should vanish would be a serious loss for the postwar haiku world.

'Let me consider it,' he said, and returned to Kyoto.

It seemed possible that both of us could sacrifice everything for haiku, but Seitō was different from me in that he had a career as a psychiatrist. Demoralized by active war duty following the repression, he had finally returned to his native land, resolved to remove the anxiety caused by haiku and to stop ignoring his family. Consequently, his desire to give up haiku was strong. By trying to draw Seitō back into haiku, I wondered if I might be a deceptive signpost at the last turning on his path.

At the mental hospital by the foot of Higashiyama, Seitō was leading a life separate from his wife and children. It was there that I visited him. As the mid-summer sun set, mosquitos buzzed, and in the distance we could hear the drumbeat of a Bon dance.

We were already middle-aged. Gazing into the face of one whose own life had also suffered much on haiku's account, Seitō said, 'I will do it, too.'

When I left for Kobe, he gave me a little sugar and some wheat flour. Carrying it with care on the crowded train, I prayed that haiku would not bring harm to his life again.

A STORY OF SOUNDING SIRENS

After I had repaid, with great difficulty, the ten thousand yen I owed C—ko after I cancelled her plans to turn my house into the 'Hillside Hotel,' I was at a complete loss as to how I could go on eating. It was just then that a man approached me about subleasing my house for his offices. He had established a company for the restoration of interior utilities such as electricity and water supply in households in war-torn Kobe. Since his employees would be mainly technicians who used to be at city hall, I rented the whole downstairs to him. I was living alone then, so I confined myself to a monkish cell at the back of the top floor.

It was in this six-tatami room that Ishida Hakyō stopped over on his first return visit to Matsuyama after the war, and where Yamamoto Kenkichi and his daughter Yasumiko from Kyoto came for an overnight visit. They ate, without complaint, simple dishes prepared with my own hands.

As soon as the company opened for business, orders began pouring in from city hall and the prefectural office, all for interior work on buildings taken over by the U.S. Armed Forces. I ended up working as chief liaison, reading order slips and negotiating with those on the job site. Finally I could breathe a sigh of relief.

Under an unbelievable autumn sky, riding in a jeep every day, I ran around the burnt-out sites of Kobe. Whether in negotiations with officers and soldiers at headquarters in the Jinko Building on the seashore, or in a workshop at the former Chamber of Commerce and Industry Building, I had the opportunity to closely observe the U.S. forces – their discipline, the relationships between officers and soldiers, feelings between blacks and whites. The Japanese military used college professors as construction laborers, but the Americans matched soldiers' duties with their civilian professions. The enlisted men, without exception, disliked the officers, but they accomplished their assigned tasks with a sense of responsibility and pride. Making excuses to these diligent soldiers and officers for the way my company's workers, battered by defeat and one step away from malnutrition, did their jobs was like a thorn in my side.

The first job I supervised was the dismantling and transfer of sirens, which had been set up on the rooftops of elementary schools, to requisitioned buildings and hotels. Nothing was written on the work order but: 'Set up sirens for emergency use on buildings A, B, C and D by such-and-such a day.'

I consulted with city hall and then proceeded to remove sirens from the rooftops of schools, but due to a worker's carelessness, things became very complicated. On close inspection I discovered that a siren is of extraordinary size, with a pedestal large enough to cover about three tatami mats. It took the technician two full days to dismantle a siren, using nonprofessional workers in a weakened condition, and then another day to carry it down to the ground. And rather than moving the sirens one by one to their new locations, he had all five carried into the basement at headquarters. After that, they became my responsibility.

The sirens had to be reassembled in the basement prior to being shipped to designated buildings for reinstallation. I was completely confounded. Neither did I know the first thing about electricity, nor had the technicians, who were close to retirement, ever seen sirens like these before. To make matters worse, the sizes of the parts for each siren were completely different. Since they had been thrown into the basement in complete disarray, the sorting out of one complete assembly required us to try out all the parts in various combinations. Moreover, since the parts were made of cast iron, it took ten men a great deal of effort to lift them; if they did not fit, the men would have to maneuver another piece into position. Even when it seemed the whole thing finally fit together onto one pedestal, we would discover that the screw mounts were in the wrong place. Nothing had been standardized.

Our men were working eight hours a day. According to the orders, five sirens were to be installed within a month. A week passed, and then ten days, yet not a single siren was completely assembled. A story by Dostoevsky tells of a group of prisoners driven to insanity by being forced to carry piles of bricks from one place to another and then back again. In the same way, temporary hired workers, already beaten down by war, were now exhausting what little vitality they had by repeatedly lifting and lowering heavy iron assemblies in the basement of a building requisitioned by the American Army, their faces becoming paler and paler day by day.

Every night I had bad dreams. The mere mention of the word 'iron' made me jump. Even after the war the air-raid sirens continued to torture me.

For the first several days, the American officers and soldiers observed us in silence, but seeing that even after three weeks we had not assembled a single siren, they tried to transfer the work to another company. Unfortunately, in those days there was no other company like ours. We were obliged at last to search for the manufacturer of the sirens. By this time, the Americans were so frustrated they would fling their caps to the floor and stamp on them, tearing their hair and roaring with anger. I was the only one who could understand their vulgarities. For some time I myself had been cursing the manufacturers, who had not bothered at all with standard parts.

And so it happened that I found myself getting out of a jeep in the fire-ravaged district of Jōtō-ku in Osaka to search for the manufacturer of the sirens, although there seemed no chance the company still existed in that vast stretch of rubble.

'If I had been the general, I wouldn't have let them bomb within two miles of this place,' the soldier muttered, kicking a scorched brick. If it had been up to me or any other Japanese, the search for the company would have ended there. However, this soldier had been given an order to 'find the company and bring the engineer in charge.' Whistling all the way, he drove the jeep first to the police station, then to a factory inspector who gave us the address of the president of the company, who in turn directed us to the home of one of the engineers.

I had never lived in Osaka, so even before it burned I would have been a geographical stranger; now that it was nothing but an expanse of scattered debris, I was unable to tell north from south, and neither could the American, but he remained unruffled. His thorough sense of responsibility impressed me as we searched for the engineer's house in vain.

Toward evening we finally located the engineer in an old air-raid shelter in the midst of the ashes of an eastern suburb of Osaka. I felt as if my legs would sink out from under me, and the soldier startled the old man with an abrupt hug.

The next morning the old engineer kindly reported to headquarters, but seeing his machinery in pieces did nothing but upset him. At that point, I was summoned before a high-ranking officer and accused of deliberate obstruction. He threatened to turn me over to the MPs.

MPs are very disagreeable, so the engineer and I stayed up all of that night, taking close measurements of those damn sirens, carefully noting the positions of the screw holes, and at dawn, there among the iron parts in the damp basement, we collapsed from exhaustion.

Two days later, we disassembled the siren that we had finally managed to build, carried it up to the roof of the building, and reassembled it. When we switched it on and the first sounds went shrieking out all over Kobe, the Americans in the building were thrown into a panic and raised a clamor like the insane. Up on the rooftop the engineer and I laughed until our stomachs ached.

It took us another three long months to set up the other four sirens. We suspect the officer in charge of the project suffered from a liver problem as a result. Even now, when I cross the Mukogawa River on the Hankyū Railway and look up at the siren there on the roof of the hotel by the sea, I have to smile a bitter smile.

Following our work with the sirens, we set about repairing elevators, including a gigantic freight elevator in the huge Mitsubishi warehouse; but it was the order to install water service on the hill at the back of Tarumi on Mount James that created the most difficulty. With the help of the city water supplier we set up relay pumps in three stages, and finally put in a supply line to the house on the mountain. After a short breather, we were told we were required to set a test fire to try out the fire pumps. Since the volume of water was the lowest allowed, this news upset us, and I insisted on being excused from the test. After this experience, I jumped whenever the American Army ran a fire engine.

Of all my jobs, the one that took the longest was the repair work for the Chamber of Commerce and Industry Building on the seashore.

The entire building had been converted into a barracks. As soon as we repaired one thing, another problem would crop up. Though it was the special technicians who actually did the work, I had to be present to assist with every type of job, be it electrical, water, or plumbing.

What caused the most trouble was the flush toilets. Big soldiers broke the foot pedals constantly, and strange things would get stuck in the drainpipes. Once when I was helping a repair, Milhorn, the intellectual soldier in the military administration department, recognized me and asked, 'Uncle, what are you doing there?' I was nonplussed. The uncle he had respected had become a toilet repairman.

Also, a Chinese soldier on duty in the barracks dining hall once saw me swishing away with a wire snake, and took the trouble to take me aside to say, 'Just because Japan lost the war, don't let yourself lose your pride in being Oriental. In America, plumbing is the lowest sort of profession.' He informed me of this with a serious face. But I wanted to try everything. A dentist, a company executive, a businessman – my jobs frequently changed, but after hearing that this was the lowest, I made a decision to stick with it. Besides, I now had a friend on the plumbing detail. Of Polish descent, Ben was a solid fellow who had been a shipbuilder; without knowing exactly when, we had become close friends. Through Ben, I came to understand how American laborers worked. Other soldiers would leave jobs unfinished when the time came, but, partly due to the nature of his job, Ben would stick with it until it was completed. When I praised him he would smile and answer, 'In order to please my friends, I always follow through.'

The way Americans went wild at Christmas seemed absurd, even though I was familiar with the tradition. When Ben drove his jeep up to my house at six o'clock that Christmas Eve and told me, his face pale, that the toilet for the hall where the Christmas Eve celebration was to be held that night was overflowing and flooding the restaurant with sewage, I was appalled. The workers had gone home; not a single one remained. Ben and I spent the next hour getting covered with sewage as we struggled to repair the trouble before the celebration began. When we finished, we shook hands – hands covered with the excrement of others.

In order not to forget this, I named the succeeding generations of my pet dogs 'Ben' – in Japanese a slightly formal term for bodily waste.

Around that time I received an order to report to the headquarters of the Australian Army, which was based in both Kure and Edajima. When I checked into it, I learned that the engine of a small launch plying between Kure and Edajima was out of order. I went to Hyōgo to negotiate with the manufacturer of the engine, and it was decided that their workers and technicians should go to the site. As this company also had a huge backlog of orders, I acquired the additional position of consultant for them as well.

In my second year of middle school, I had gone on a school excursion to the Edajima Naval Academy. Although it was natural for things to have changed, the profound differences in Edajima on my second visit surprised me. The school building remained undamaged, but in the wide schoolyard a young Indian soldier was wandering about, holding a poetry or some such book and a wooden plaque which read: 'Planted by the hand of the Imperial Highness.' The plaque had been discarded when the tree was chopped down.

I found the Australian military, who were using the classrooms for their offices, taking afternoon tea in proper British fashion. Yet the appointments for these rooms were worlds removed from those of the American Army. Instead of shaded desk lamps, a naked light bulb was suspended from pieces of a wooden crate nailed to the ceiling. I had lived in a British colony when I was in my late twenties, and I was used to dealing with this culture. The British, even their children, wish to be treated as gentlemen.

Riding the launch that had motor trouble, we came and went many times between Kure and Edajima, and before long the trouble was corrected. During these trips I had a conversation with the soldier who steered the launch. I discovered that he was on a quest for Vaseline which, according to him, did not exist in the treatment rooms of the Australian Army.

'To tell the truth,' he said, 'I got really annoyed. When I substituted toothpaste, it felt too cold. So I tried using shaving cream, but when it bubbled I got slapped on the face.'

The use for the Vaseline was plain enough. I took a second look at his great physical size and could not help but laugh. Even this advisor for the diesel engine manufacturing company did not have any Vaseline. Later, I had it sent out by the case from a company in Kobe.

The job in Kure completed, I happened to change trains at Hiroshima on my way back to Kobe, and from the desolation of the ruined station I went alone into the city at night.

In the cloudy sky there was neither moon nor stars, and across the pitch-black earth a dank autumnal wind was blowing. As I walked, groping for direction, an ashen-faced woman approached, speaking a word or two. Her lips appeared pitch-black, probably from a thick application of rouge. When I remained silent, she passed by with a grunt. Sitting on a stone by the side of the road, I took out a boiled egg and slowly peeled the shell, unexpectedly shocked by the smooth surface of the egg. With a flash of searing incandescence, the skins of human beings had as easily slipped off all over this city. To eat a boiled egg in the wind of that black night, I was forced to open my mouth. In that moment, this haiku came to me:

> Hiroshima –
> to eat a boiled egg,
> a mouth opens

A horse with a drooping head passed before me. Did it notice me there in the dark? It breathed heavily through its nose. Was it really a horse?

From the distance the wind came sighing, thin as the sound of humans weeping. The summer before, the stone on which I sat had turned to fire. There had been murder on a massive scale, beyond comprehension. The survivors had walked in great sluggish lines, the skin trailing from their arms. I could still hear their feet shuffling closer, closer …

I stood up in the darkness and, taking a step, bumped into the corpse of a pine tree which was still standing. Somewhere the sound of water could be heard, probably from a broken supply line. I found myself terribly thirsty. No moon, no stars. There was nothing. All that there was, was a dark night. Human beings, in order to kill other human beings, had created this thing. And I, too, was a human being.

'Nihilism,' whispered my heart, and the same heart smiled with derision. Such sentiments did not exist here. Not American or British, not Soviet or Japanese, but the full scope of human evil cut me to the bone. Taking the midnight train from Hiroshima station, I returned to Kobe, where there was sunshine, autumn-colored mountains, the deep sea, people alive and walking about. It was next to impossible to imagine the land of Hiroshima I had seen the previous night lying not so distant from Kobe.

LIKE A ROLLING STONE

Of all the orders we received from the American Army, the most difficult ones were, as I mentioned before, the siren project and the project to supply water to Mount James; but in a different sense the one which troubled me most was the job of removing water from the basement of Building A out near the beach.

Near the beachfront in Kobe, which was reclaimed long ago from the sea, water is sure to seep into basements. The pressure of ground water has a power beyond the imagination; if the foundation of a building has been imperfectly built, the basement is a pond all year long.

The work order read: 'Within ten days the water in the basement of the five-story Building A should be removed.' When I asked an engineer in the company about this, he told me that it would be difficult to do even within a month because the foundation was constructed in such a slipshod way that it was bound to leak through in one place if it was stopped up in another. If we tried to keep up with the water, we would clearly become exhausted. Coming and going many times a day between headquarters and the job site, I cursed the war, the world, the water, and the very ground itself. The reasons for cursing were countless.

When I asked an officer what the building was being requisitioned for, he gave no answer other than, 'None of your business.' The officer in charge was a young gentleman, and though he sometimes became angry, he would never say 'Goddamn.' The worst that came out of his mouth was, 'Darn so-and-so.' Though he refused to answer my question, I sensed a momentary discomfort in his expression.

'Something's fishy,' I thought to myself, and began to pay careful attention.

In any case, even after the electrical work for the whole building had been completed, the basement remained a pond. The pump ran day and night. Workers were assigned to the night shift, but the influx of discolored water continued unabated. Finally, unable to wait any longer, headquarters began moving wooden beds into each room.

'Why then, it's a barracks, is it?' I thought, but the expression on the officer's face did not fit that explanation.

On a day when the autumn winds came blowing in from the sea, driving fallen leaves along the pavement, the 'barracks' was opened. It turned out to be a brothel run for the military. The women had been gathered by an 'expert' who had been running a whorehouse before the war; there seemed to be at least one hundred and fifty of them.

White soldiers and black soldiers were kept in separate barracks, and so it was that each group turned up at P House on alternate days.

Those who came early in the morning sprang into action at about eight o'clock and then got roaring drunk as if they owned the world. I was reminded of the Chinese proverb: 'Liquor pond surrounded by flesh forest,' but this whole building was becoming more like a zoo, with white monkeys and black monkeys running amok on alternate days.

At the entrance on the first floor an MP stood with dignity, but the beasts inside destroyed equipment, not just the electrical installations and toilets, but anything they could lay their hands on. The workers and I would have nothing to do with a problem unless there was a work order, not even if an electrical cord sparked before our eyes, or a toilet was plugged and sewage was flowing into the corridor. Even if we repaired something in the morning, the drunkards would break it in the afternoon. What was the use?

Finally, the engineering officer in charge gave up, stating that I should take responsibility to repair whatever I could, no matter what it was, no matter what time it was, and that he would provide me with blank work orders. By virtue of this arrangement, the master repairman with the mustache was obliged both day and night to take his workmen and venture into the garden of beasts.

Basically, American soldiers looked well-dressed and well-fed. In the requisitioned Chamber of Commerce and Industry Building, even a former oil-field worker from Texas was lodged in a room with a crimson carpet. Yet these same men indiscriminately destroyed flush toilets. Finally, the officer in charge lost his temper and had toilets built outside along the seashore in a traditional Japanese design called *kawaya*. The soldiers had to sit in a line with their buttocks hanging out over the sea, without benefit of partitions or doors.

They behaved like barbarians. Even though we could see them – stark-naked and hairy, doing things we'd seen only on picture postcards from Paris – they were able to ignore us completely. There was an unobstructed view of all five beds in each room, and on each was ensconced one of our women. A young technical worker, seeing this for the first time, fled back into the corridor and threw up. I was beyond hostility, having developed a dislike for the human animal itself.

No matter how much time passed, the underground water did not abate. One chilly night while making an inspection tour, I discovered the pump-tending workman staring dejectedly at the dirty water. Since the flush toilets broke daily, urine became intermixed with the ground water. There were no words of consolation for the young man who had to tend the pumps all night long in the basement of a whorehouse.

On the floors above the free-for-all never ceased. Each time there was a fight the MP ran upstairs and gave both sides a good whaling with a white stick. Over the matter of women, there were conflicts even between whites and blacks, and at such times both sides fought in groups. Some fellows were stabbed to death. I suppose that is why they finally closed the whorehouse. Still, the job of dealing with underground water continued.

Just as the tide ebbs, the women dispersed in all directions. One night, after having dinner with the officer in charge, we descended into the basement of the building, where there was now only a watchman, to check on the amount of water welling up at night. The usual young technical worker was there in a dark, cold corner, and sitting on an empty box next to him was a young woman with downcast eyes. Though it was already November, she was wearing a faded summer dress.

The officer winked at me. I, too, assumed the technician had called a prostitute. Should I scold a worker who did such things during his shift? After all, I worked only as the liaison, definitely not as the chief engineer.

The officer was watching my demeanor with a smug kind of grin, as if he were anticipating a glimpse into the conduct between Japanese at times such as this. Because I had felt a deep sympathy for this young man for quite some time now, I simply asked him for an explanation. He told me that the woman had been working since summer on the floor above, and that when the building was closed she had become homeless.

After hearing this, I noticed on the woman's lap a piece of the bread my company provided its workers for a late-night meal. In those days, no matter what kind of a woman she was, as long as she was a woman, there was no danger of starvation. Yet, while the other one hundred and forty-nine had gone, this girl, wearing only thin summer clothing, sat on a wooden box in a cold, dank basement, slowly chewing a crumbling piece of the bread.

The young worker made an effort not to look at the officer's face.

'This person says she can't stand her business any longer, and since she has nowhere to go, she has been coming here only at night and sleeping in the pumproom next door. I guess this is probably her third day.' So saying, he smiled faintly. I knew that he was living at his aunt's house in Osaka. His daily wages barely covered food and transportation expenses. Up to then, I had avoided asking if he was a demobilized soldier; it would not have been right for an ex-Japanese soldier to do this job.

Hearing my explanation, the officer could only stare at the dejected-looking pair. Then he placed an entire bag of American tobacco on the youth's lap. After that he called me into the pumproom to inspect the machinery. He coughed continually, a dry hacking cough, which he blamed on the moisture in the basement.

The next night the youth did not report for work. The girl also disappeared. I have no idea what became of them.

By that time I had again begun to write and publish haiku. Through Wada Hensuirō, I met Hashimoto Takako of Ayame Ike in Nara. One day when I went to see her, we called on Seitō together. That day we looked at a manuscript of Seishi's haiku collection, *Gekirō* (Turbulent Waves), which he had given Mrs. Hashimoto for safekeeping.

'Seishi Sensei might scold me for showing you this,' she said.

All of us who saw the manuscript were deeply impressed. During those five years of war, while Seitō and I had kept our distance from haiku because we feared the government authorities, the master had continued to work every day with unremitting zeal, sometimes recording as many as ten poems in a single day. The change in style from his collection *Shichiyō* also surprised us. After reading the manuscript, Seitō and I accidentally caught one another's eye. At that moment our commitment to writing haiku was sealed.

In order to found the new periodical *Tenrō*, I found that I spent a great deal of time traveling to Tokyo. So, since my company was doing well, I resigned. My income was now derived solely from subleasing my three rooms.

Originally, the house on Yamamoto Street had been managed by the aunt of the owner, who had gone to war. When the property taxes had come due, she had asked me to buy it. I was unable to, and it was eventually sold through a broker to a Chinese man, after which I was pressured every day to move out.

In those days, most of the houses in Kobe which remained standing were bought up by the Chinese. When only Japanese people are involved, it can take two or even three years for a house to be vacated; thus, a house inhabited by people who were renting could be purchased cheaply. However, when the Chinese bought such a house, they employed an 'eviction man,' who was also Chinese and who acted as proxy for the owner. He would come to live under the same roof with the Japanese tenants, making noise day and night by playing mah-jong, and invading the privacy of whatever rooms he pleased. It invariably came to the point where the Japanese could not stand it anymore and fled.

Since I was aware of this, I explained the situation to the company to which I was subleasing, and we decided to leave in return for a small compensation to cover moving expenses. But the fact was that I had nowhere to go. Before eviction day, a haiku poet who had visited me frequently from his home beyond Akashi said that I could move to his neighborhood. Since he wanted me to edit a haiku magazine he was planning to start, it seemed like a good idea. The time had finally come to leave the Kobe I so loved.

I assumed that he had already found a new home for me, but then he appeared in Kobe the day before I was to leave and suggested that we start looking for a place. Over the next few hours I felt terribly helpless, but by that evening I was able to rent a detached room in a stately mansion located in the seaside village of Befu. The next day I moved in.

Once again I was in a situation where money and I were strangers, but *Tenrō* had been founded and published by Yōtokusha in Tenri City, so with the editing fee I was managing to scrape by.

While all this was happening, Kinuyo, who had been raising our child in Kyushu, had returned to Kobe. Our child was now four years old.

Fortunately, Kinuyo had an inner strength forged by poverty. When the firewood was used up, she would go down to the beach and pick up driftwood, wrap it in a kerchief, and carry it home on her back. When there was nothing left to eat with the rice, she would dig clams and serve them to us boiled. It was winter by then, and the vast stretch of the Banshū plain was a solid, withered color.

My head always seemed about to burst with ideas for the newly founded *Tenrō*, as well as with thoughts for my own haiku-writing activity, so there was no room left to dwell on the poverty of my home. I had been obsessed with haiku since 1934. Because of the repression I had taken a five-year break, but now poetry emerged again with explosive force. It was a tremendously heady sensation, but I also felt suffocated by it.

So I began setting aside one or two hours a day in which to forget haiku completely. I began fishing. While sitting at the edge of a brook running through muddy rice fields and simply concentrating on my float, my inner plains became vast and vacant – I became like water.

Passing along the rice-drying racks covered with morning dew, I would squat at the edge of an irrigation ditch and scoop out shrimp to use as bait. My fishing spot was by a brook where seawater flowed, so I could catch both large freshwater Prussian carp and sea gobies.

When evening came, smoke would ascend here and there over the far-off fields, and shrikes would cry out. In the north along the mountains, a train would slowly pass from left to right, sometimes disappearing into the woods and emerging again.

My haiku was now different from what it had been before the war. The new haiku was attended by the quiet shadow of death.

> My death approaching
> from edge to edge, a train
> through a withered field

Some days later, I went up to Tokyo on business and called on Akimoto Fujio in Yokohama. It was our custom to show one another our haiku poems, so I shared this poem with him.

Fujio stared at this haiku for some time, then slowly he

opened his own haiku notebook. It was a commonplace exercise book like one his school-aged son used, and its cover bore Fujio's characteristic aphorisms, such as 'Value the concrete' and 'A steady gaze.' Fujio pointed silently to a haiku that read:

> My death approaching –
> crossing the withered field,
> a chain of trains.

We looked at each other for awhile, then began laughing at the same time. We had trouble stopping.

Though there are such things as similar haiku, or similar images, this was too close. Indeed, the phrase used by both Fujio and me, 'my death approaching,' was unique, used in haiku for the first time. Though metaphysically the two poems reflected the same idea, the true feelings behind the actual language were more personal, and so we discussed this at some length.

We were only one year apart in age, had both devoted ourselves to the New Rising Haiku movement, and though in different jails, we had eaten the same rotten prison food. After the war we both belonged to *Tenrō* and even shared a common ideal regarding haiku. Wondering if such factors could explain the coincidence of the poems – even though we were separated by the distance between Yokohama and Hyōgo prefecture – I thought to myself, 'This is certainly dangerous.'

My life in the seaside village continued for ten months, during which time my modest self-edited magazine *Gekirō* failed. I was putting my heart and soul into *Tenrō*; there was no time to devote to anything else.

Since Nagata Kōi was living in a neighboring town, we would call on one another. He had deep, strong eyes, and always spoke eloquently. It was never just talk; he always had something to say.

My quiet life on the plain by the sea ended as a result of my friend Seitō's distress at my poverty. He got me a job at the hospital run by the Women's Medical College.

Through the withered fields, I moved eastward with my few belongings and began a new life, overlooking the Yodogawa plain.

Eight years later I returned to Tokyo. Since I first left Tokyo to settle in Kobe in 1942, I had been moving like a rolling stone. Fourteen years had slipped away.

TRANSLATOR'S ACKNOWLEDGMENTS

The Kobe Hotel: Memoirs is a revised edition of my translation of Sanki's two sets of prose memoirs *Kobe* and *Kobe Sequel*. The earlier versions of these translations originally appeared, along with a selection of Sanki's haiku, in *The Kobe Hotel*, published by Weatherhill in 1993.

While preparing the original Weatherhill edition, I received valuable aid from Susan Wright and Meg Taylor, both of whom edited the entire manuscript, including its haiku section.

My sincere gratitude goes to Paul Rossiter who gave me valuable feedback regarding my revisions for the new Isobar edition.

Finally, my thanks are due to Saitō Tomoko, my mother, who kept a library which included modern Japanese literature on her bookshelves. One of the volumes was a collection of haiku and tanka. As a young boy, I would open the book again and again. I was particularly intrigued by Sanki's haiku. Without this experience, which later led me to read Sanki's prose work, this book might not have come to fruition.

Masaya Saito
2023